Language Arts
Workbook

Siegfried Engelmann
Bonnie Grossen
Steve Osborn

Acknowledgments

Greatest appreciation and thanks to Debbi Kleppen and Cally Dwyer for their very knowledgeable assistance preparing the manuscript and their extra effort in preparing the field test version. Many thanks to the Arthur Academy, Isaac Eivers and his students, and Angie Obrist for field testing this version of the program. Thanks to John Weber, Ashley Vanderwall and Ann Arbogast in assisting with the data retrieval from the field testing.

mheducation.com/prek-12

Copyright © 2021 McGraw-Hill Education

All rights reserved. No part of this publication may be reproduced or distributed in any form or by any means, or stored in a database or retrieval system, without the prior written consent of McGraw-Hill Education, including, but not limited to, network storage or transmission, or broadcast for distance learning.

Send all inquiries to:
McGraw-Hill Education
8787 Orion Place
Columbus, OH 43240

ISBN: 978-0-07-905383-1
MHID: 0-07-905383-1

Printed in the United States of America.

1 2 3 4 5 6 7 8 9 LMN 24 23 22 21 20

A IDENTIFY SUBJECT AND PREDICATE

> A complete sentence always has two parts—a part that names and a part that tells more.
> The part that names is the **subject**.
> The part that tells more is the **predicate**.

Circle the subject and underline the predicate in the sentences.

1. They wrote five sentences.

2. A large room had lots of video games.

3. Mrs. Brown kept throwing the ball to her dog.

4. He smiles.

5. The Jones family tries to stay in good health.

6. Liz and her dog ran three miles every morning.

7. The oldest car in town belongs to Mr. Frost.

8. The best dog in the show is a collie.

Lesson 1

B TEST FOR A NOUN

- Words in sentences have different parts of speech.
- Some words are nouns. There are different ways to test for whether words are nouns.
- Here's one test: If the word makes sense with the word **one** or the word **some** in front of it, it's a noun.

Examples: beautiful   situation   sand   people

Test each word to see if it's a noun. If it is a noun, circle the word <u>one</u> or <u>some</u>. If it is not a noun, circle <u>not a noun</u>.

1. milk	one	some	not a noun
2. quickly	one	some	not a noun
3. happy	one	some	not a noun
4. argument	one	some	not a noun
5. water	one	some	not a noun
6. seeds	one	some	not a noun
7. hungry	one	some	not a noun
8. always	one	some	not a noun
9. events	one	some	not a noun
10. noise	one	some	not a noun
11. if	one	some	not a noun
12. old	one	some	not a noun
13. sister	one	some	not a noun

C USE PRECISE LANGUAGE

> Words that are more general tell about more things.
> Words that are more specific tell about fewer things.
> a. houses   buildings
> b. people   girls
> c. cars   vehicles
> d. appliances   refrigerators
> e. bottles   containers

Circle the more specific word.

1. bottles   containers   5. houses   buildings
2. vehicles   cars   6. bottles   milk bottles
3. appliances   refrigerators   7. trucks   vehicles
4. people   girls

D Write the past tense for these verbs.

	Present	Past
1.	smell, smells	
2.	walk, walks	
3.	study, studies	
4.	has	
5.	have	
6.	is	
7.	am	
8.	are	
9.	fall, falls	
10.	think, thinks	
11.	buy, buys	

END OF LESSON 1

2 Name _____

A Test each word to see if it's a noun. If it is a noun, circle the word <u>one</u> or <u>some</u>. If it is not a noun, circle <u>not a noun</u>.

1. slowly   one   some   not a noun
2. dream   one   some   not a noun
3. happy   one   some   not a noun
4. stories   one   some   not a noun
5. not   one   some   not a noun
6. willing   one   some   not a noun
7. turkey   one   some   not a noun
8. lonely   one   some   not a noun
9. stupid   one   some   not a noun
10. racket   one   some   not a noun

B Circle the subject and underline the predicate in the sentences.

1. The yellow print is hard to read.
2. The car had new brakes.
3. The blue car did not have new paint.
4. My aunt loves watermelon.
5. Those boys like to play baseball.
6. They were happy.
7. An old gray goose was on the road.
8. She likes ice cream.

C USE PRECISE LANGUAGE

> Words that are more general tell about more things.
> Words that are more specific tell about fewer things.
>
> a. pets   cats
> b. games   card games
> c. trees   plants
> d. shoes   clothes
> e. insects   beetles

Circle the more specific word.

1. insects   beetles   4. trees   plants

2. clothes   shoes   5. trees   firs

3. cats   pets   6. games   card games

D Write the past tense for these verbs.

	Present	Past
1.	smell, smells	
2.	walk, walks	
3.	study, studies	
4.	has	
5.	have	
6.	is	
7.	am	
8.	are	
9.	fall, falls	
10.	think, thinks	
11.	buy, buys	

END OF LESSON 2

A. Circle the subject and underline the predicate in the sentences.

1. His mother drinks a lot of water.
2. She was doing her homework.
3. The woman who lives next door has a parrot and a cat.
4. We stayed up late and watched TV.
5. Mr. Barker and my dad baked desserts in our oven.
6. We played with his brother and his cousin.

B. Write the past tense for these verbs.

	Present	Past
1.	smell, smells	
2.	walk, walks	
3.	study, studies	
4.	has	
5.	have	
6.	is	
7.	am	
8.	are	
9.	fall, falls	
10.	think, thinks	
11.	buy, buys	

END OF LESSON 3

Name _____

A Circle the subject and underline the predicate in the sentences.

1. They hid many things in the attic.

2. Rhonda and her brother continued to argue.

3. The largest dam on the river is 30 miles from Roseberg.

4. Fixing that roof is expensive.

5. The richest man in town is 94 years old.

6. His oldest daughter is studying medicine.

B Write the present forms for these verbs.

	Present	Past
1.		smelled
2.		walked
3.		studied
4.		had
5.		was
6.		were
7.		fell
8.		thought
9.		bought

END OF LESSON 4

5

A Circle the subject and underline the predicate of each sentence.

1. The man in the brown coat lives next to Millie.

2. Our rent has gone up three times in one year.

3. The owner of that car is only 16 years old.

4. It was very cold out.

5. My phone line can handle three calls at once.

6. Sticks and stones may break my bones.

7. Weighing all the puppies was difficult.

B Write a sentence that is more specific than either sentence shown by using parts of those sentences.

Item 1: A. The man in the gray coat had some money.
         B. He had $34.25.

Item 2: A. They went to Jim Franklin's house.
         B. Three boys went to his house.

Item 3: A. The car belongs to the people who live across the street.
         B. The car with a flat tire belongs to neighbors.

Item 4: A. She cleaned Amy's teeth.
         B. The dental hygienist cleaned them.

Item 5: A. They are reptiles with no legs.
         B. Snakes are animals with no legs.

Lesson 5

C REPLACE A NOUN PHRASE WITH A PRONOUN

You've learned about nouns.

A noun with its adjectives may be replaced by a **pronoun. Pronouns are more general words than nouns.**

Here are some common pronouns that are used only in the predicate: **him, her, them, us, me.**

Other pronouns used in the predicate are: **it, you.**

> **Tom went with his friends.**
> **Tom went with them.**
>
> **Tom went to the store.**
> **Tom went to it.**

Remember, a pronoun is a **more general word** that **replaces a noun and its adjectives.** It's more general because it can be used to refer to more things than the noun refers to.

D Cross out the last two words of each sentence and write a pronoun to replace them.

1. John walked with his cane.

2. The engine of the train pulled 15 cars.

3. Don had an argument with his sister.

4. Frank drank cold water.

5. Mr. Jackson fixed large hamburgers.

6. Mrs. Taylor was proud of her son.

E. Write the past tense form.

	Present	Past
1.	see, sees	
2.	catch, catches	
3.	teach, teaches	
4.	lose, loses	
5.	write, writes	
6.	come, comes	
7.	feel, feels	
8.	hear, hears	
9.	know, knows	
10.	stand, stands	

INDEPENDENT WORK

F. Write the past tense verb.

	Present	Past
1.	smell, smells	
2.	walk, walks	
3.	study, studies	
4.	has	
5.	have	
6.	is	
7.	am	
8.	are	
9.	fall, falls	
10.	think, thinks	
11.	buy, buys	

END OF LESSON 5

6

A IDENTIFY PAST OR PRESENT TENSE

You know that all sentences have a verb. The verb may be one word or more than one word.

1. She **walked** fast.
2. She **has walked** fast.
3. She **has been walking** fast.

The first verb word is always the **key verb.** The key verb tells **past** or **present** tense.

1. He **has seen** those boys.
2. He **has eaten** tuna.
3. We **have shopped** at Z-Mart many times.
4. She **is walking** fast.
5. I **am walking** fast.
6. We **were walking** fast.
7. We **had played** all day.

B Circle the key verb. Circle past or present to tell about the key verb in all the items.

	Actor(s)	Verb	Other Words		
1.		have been looking		past	present
2.		were riding		past	present
3.		have been going		past	present
4.		is wondering		past	present
5.		had bought		past	present
6.		am seeing		past	present
7.		have been shopping		past	present

C. Write the past tense form.

	Present	Past
1.	see, sees	
2.	catch, catches	
3.	teach, teaches	
4.	lose, loses	
5.	write, writes	
6.	come, comes	
7.	feel, feels	
8.	hear, hears	
9.	know, knows	
10.	stand, stands	

INDEPENDENT WORK

D. Circle the subject and underline the predicate of each sentence.

1. The heaviest book weighed almost six pounds.

2. His third son was the tallest of all his children.

3. Nothing made him laugh more than a good clown.

4. The person with the tallest hat had spent a lot of money.

5. Reports told us about the approaching storm.

6. Five of the seven crew members had been in the Navy.

7. Everything was a lie.

END OF LESSON 6

Name _____

A Write the present-tense forms of these verbs.

	Present	Past
1.		saw
2.		caught
3.		taught
4.		lost
5.		wrote
6.		came
7.		felt
8.		heard
9.		knew
10.		stood

B IDENTIFY KEY VERB POSITION

His brother was playing outside.

Rule: The first word of the predicate is the key verb.

a. His brother was ten years old.
b. The largest bird could eat a lot of berries.
c. Rowing boats can be very difficult.

C Circle the subject and underline the predicate of each sentence. Label the key verb **KV**.

1. Three cats were fighting over some food.

2. They were talking for hours.

3. His youngest daughter had a birthday last week.

4. Five greeting cards fell from the table.

5. Joe and I have been pals for a very long time.

D Circle the key verb. Circle past or present to tell about the key verb in all the items.

	Actor(s)	Verb	Other Words		
1.		are walking		past	present
2.		walked		past	present
3.		study		past	present
4.		are learning		past	present
5.		were considering		past	present
6.		have seen		past	present
7.		thought		past	present
8.		is working		past	present

END OF LESSON 7

Name _____

A MOVE PART OF THE PREDICATE

Regular sentence: **They played** *before* **school began.**

Sentence with part of the predicate moved to the beginning of the sentence: **Before school began, they played.**

B Rewrite these sentences so they start with the *italicized* word. Put a comma after the part moved.

1. She found a bird nest *in* the corner of the room.
   _____

2. The birds chirped *before* the sun came up.
   _____

3. The air smelled fresh *after* the rain.
   _____

4. You will become a good musician *if* you practice daily.
   _____

5. They were still working *when* the sun set.
   _____

Lesson 8

C Circle the subject of each sentence. Circle <u>one</u> or <u>more than one</u> to indicate how many are in the subject.

1. Tammy and I have always known that.

    one   more than one

2. The best things in life are free.

    one   more than one

3. The damage is quite extensive.

    one   more than one

4. No house was completely destroyed in the fire.

    one   more than one

5. Tammy has always known that.

    one   more than one

6. The horse was jumping and snorting all day long.

    one   more than one

7. That work has been very tiring and tedious.

    one   more than one

8. We have been living on Thorn Street 5 years.

    one   more than one

D Circle the subject and underline the key verb (KV). Circle past or present to indicate the tense of the key verb.

1. My mother and her best friend were having a loud argument.

   past   present

2. Herb and I have worked on the same school project.

   past   present

3. My tablet needs charging.

   past   present

4. The longest line shows the number of people.

   past   present

5. The girl with the pony tail is out of style.

   past   present

6. They were spending more money than before.

   past   present

INDEPENDENT WORK

E Circle the key verb. Circle past or present indicate the tense of the key verb in each item.

	Actor(s)	Verb	Other Words		
1.		have been talking		past	present
2.		are walking		past	present
3.		have studied		past	present
4.		learn		past	present
5.		were considering		past	present

F Write the present-tense forms of these verbs.

	Present	Past
1.		saw
2.		caught
3.		taught
4.		lost
5.		wrote
6.		came
7.		felt
8.		heard
9.		knew
10.		stood

END OF LESSON 8

Name _____

A Circle the subject of each sentence. Circle <u>one</u> or <u>more than one</u> to indicate how many are in the subject.

1. Three babies cry all night long.

   one   more than one

2. The painting sells for a lot of money.

   one   more than one

3. The baby cries to be fed.

   one   more than one

4. He talks for hours.

   one   more than one

5. Five men from town talk every day on the phone.

   one   more than one

6. Joe and I want to go.

   one   more than one

B Circle the key verb. Circle <u>one</u>, <u>more than one</u>, or <u>either</u> to describe the subject of the sentence.

	Actor(s)	Verb	Other Words			
1.		runs		one	more than one	either
2.		ran		one	more than one	either
3.		look		one	more than one	either
4.		were riding		one	more than one	either
5.		has swum		one	more than one	either
6.		is wondering		one	more than one	either
7.		bought		one	more than one	either
8.		have been seen		one	more than one	either
9.		stops		one	more than one	either
10.		was		one	more than one	either
11.		are climbing		one	more than one	either

C **Circle the subject. Underline the key verb. Circle past or present tell about the key verb.**

1. (Paul) has <u>finished</u> his homework.
   　　　　past　　　present

2. (We) were <u>watching</u> an interesting program.
   　　　　past　　　present

3. The (girls) have been <u>telling</u> secrets to each other.
   　　　　past　　　present

4. The (sailboat) is <u>tipping</u> over.
   　　　　past　　　present

5. That (fish) <u>smells</u> rotten.
   　　　　past　　　present

6. (They) have <u>bought</u> a lot of groceries.
   　　　　past　　　present

7. Our (mother) was busy <u>cleaning</u> the kitchen this morning.
   　　　　past　　　present

8. The (workers) <u>were</u> tired.
   　　　　past　　　present

9. The (train) has been <u>making</u> four stops every day.
   　　　　past　　　present

10. (Bees) are <u>buzzing</u> among the flowers.
   　　　　past　　　present

END OF LESSON 9

10 Name _____

A Circle the key verb. Circle *one*, *more than one*, or *either* to describe the subject of the sentence.

Actor(s)	Verb	Other Words			
1. ▓▓▓	were watching	▓▓▓	one	more than one	either
2. ▓▓▓	wandered	▓▓▓	one	more than one	either
3. ▓▓▓	look	▓▓▓	one	more than one	either
4. ▓▓▓	is writing	▓▓▓	one	more than one	either
5. ▓▓▓	found	▓▓▓	one	more than one	either
6. ▓▓▓	is working	▓▓▓	one	more than one	either

B Circle the subject and underline the key verb. Circle *past* or *present* to indicate the tense the key verb.

1. Time is passing us by.

   past   present

2. I have never said that.

   past   present

3. Joey felt cold.

   past   present

4. Mia and Tia are sisters.

   past   present

5. The campfire burned all night long.

   past   present

22 Lesson 10

C Write the past-tense verb.

	Present	Past
1.	may	
2.	can	
3.	shall	
4.	do, does	
5.	choose, chooses	
6.	fly, flies	
7.	go, goes	
8.	sit, sits	
9.	run, runs	
10.	sell, sells	
11.	tell, tells	

INDEPENDENT WORK

D Write the past-tense verb.

	Present	Past
1.	see, sees	
2.	catch, catches	
3.	teach, teaches	
4.	lose, loses	
5.	write, writes	
6.	come, comes	
7.	feel, feels	
8.	hear, hears	
9.	know, knows	
10.	stand, stands	

E Circle the key verb. Circle past or present indicate the tense of the key verb in each item.

	Actor(s)	Verb	Other Words		
1.		are thinking		past	present
2.		is wishing		past	present
3.		had reviewed		past	present
4.		understands		past	present
5.		was		past	present

F Circle the subject of each sentence. Circle one or more than one to indicate how many are in the subject.

1. My dad's work clothes are worn out.

        one   more than one

2. Yesterday flew by.

        one   more than one

3. Maurice and Clarence have been saving for new bikes.

        one   more than one

4. The best tacos were from Tiki's.

        one   more than one

5. Moriah tells great stories.

        one   more than one

END OF LESSON 10

A Write the past-tense verb.

	Present	Past
1.	may	
2.	can	
3.	shall	
4.	do, does	
5.	choose, chooses	
6.	fly, flies	
7.	go, goes	
8.	sit, sits	
9.	run, runs	
10.	sell, sells	
11.	tell, tells	

B Draw a line above the joining word. Circle the subjects. Underline the key verbs. Circle past or present to indicate the tense of the key verbs.

> These words can join two sentences together:
>
> **when   where   while   why**
>
> **When:** We were walking to school **when** the sun was coming up over the hills.
>
> **Where:** We planned to go **where** he told us.
>
> **While:** The children slept **while** the trains were clanking down the track.

1. Dejay knows why those birds make so much noise.   past   present

2. John was carrying his backpack when he saw the car turn left.   past   present

3. She can understand why her brother has two cars.   past   present

4. She knows where the fishing is good.   past   present

5. Her aunt is singing while she gets dressed.   past   present

Lesson 11

C IDENTIFY COMPLETE SENTENCE PARTS

> These verb forms are never key verbs:
> (*verb* + ing)   walking, singing, following, ringing
> (to *verb*)   to walk, to sing
>   I want to walk home.
>   I like to sing.
>
>   a. to want
>   b. want
>   c. wanting
>   d. ring
>   e. ringing
>   f. to go

For each item, circle yes or no to indicate if the item is a complete sentence. If the item is a complete sentence, circle the subject and underline the key verb.

1. Sifui and I are always singing.   Yes   No

2. Sifui and I always singing.   Yes   No

3. The horse jumping and snorting all day long.   Yes   No

4. Was jumping and snorting all day long.   Yes   No

5. Wanting to walk home.   Yes   No

6. The workers finished in a week.   Yes   No

7. To whistle while working.   Yes   No

D INTERJECTIONS

> Interjections express bursts of emotion. Interjections can be a word or a group of words. Here are some interjections:
>
> How wonderful!
> Oh really!
> What a nice bicycle!
> Wow!
> That food is delicious!
> Yum!
>
> To show strong emotion, you use an exclamation mark: !
> How in the world did you do that?
> For questions, always use a question mark: ?

Write a period (.), question mark (?), or exclamation mark (!) at the end of each item. Use an exclamation mark if the item shows strong emotion.

1. I cooked dinner for the family
2. The mashed potatoes were great
3. How can that be
4. Did you see the movie
5. Yum
6. He will give you a ride
7. Stop wasting so much water
8. That's a fantastic score
9. Are you out of your mind

END OF LESSON 11

12 Name _____

A Circle the subject and underline the key verb in each complete sentence. Circle <u>yes</u> or <u>no</u> to indicate if the item is a complete sentence.

1. Children play in the ball field.　　　　　　　　　　Yes　　No

2. Play in the gymnasium.　　　　　　　　　　　　　Yes　　No

3. The dogs were howling all night long.　　　　　　　Yes　　No

4. The dogs howling and barking all night long.　　　　Yes　　No

5. To write a long essay.　　　　　　　　　　　　　 Yes　　No

6. Cleaning the school grounds.　　　　　　　　　　 Yes　　No

7. We are cleaning.　　　　　　　　　　　　　　　 Yes　　No

B Circle the key verb. Circle <u>one</u>, <u>more than one</u>, or <u>either</u> to describe the subject of the sentence.

	Actor(s)	Verb	Other words
1.		sells	
2.		hear	
3.		had been seen	
4.		has purchased	

1. one　more than one　either
2. one　more than one　either
3. one　more than one　either
4. one　more than one　either

C — USE CONSISTENT VERB TENSE

> These words can join two sentences together:
> | | | | |
> |---|---|---|---|
> | when | where | while | why |
> | before | after | until | |
>
> You see the lightning before you hear the thunder.

Draw a line above the joining word. Circle the subjects. Underline the key verbs. Circle past or present to indicate the tense of the key verbs.

1. The birds chirped before the sun came up.   past   present

2. Our team can never win until we play good defense.   past   present

3. Grandpa's back hurts when it rains.   past   present

4. He was tired after he walked to school.   past   present

5. He knew why he did not hear the alarm.   past   present

D — Write a period (.), question mark (?), or exclamation mark (!) at the end of each item. Use an exclamation mark if the item shows strong emotion.

> Remember, interjections are bursts of emotion. To show strong emotion, you use an exclamation mark: !

1. What a beautiful dog

2. How did you know

3. That was just terrible

4. Wow

5. They were happy to be here

END OF LESSON 12

13

Name _____

A Write the present tense for these verbs.

	Present	Past
1.		might
2.		could
3.		should
4.		did
5.		chose
6.		flew

	Present	Past
7.		went
8.		sat
9.		ran
10.		sold
11.		told

B USE CONSISTENT VERB TENSE

You know that some combined sentences are made up of two complete sentence parts joined by these words:

when   where   while   why   before   after   until

A complete sentence part has a subject and a key verb.

The players have won many games after losing so many. ____
         past   present

The weather was terrible after we returned from the beach. ____
    past   present

Draw a line above the joining word in each item. Circle the subjects. Underline the key verbs. Write the number of complete sentence parts on the line. Then circle the tense past or present.

1. They were sitting near the stream when it started to rain. ____

    past   present

2. I know why Andy is in a bad mood today. ____

    past   present

3. Jenny lost her wallet after the long motorcycle ride. ____

    past   present

4. Our class completed a large project before they went on a field trip. ____

    past   present

5. We can paint the door before the trim. ____

    past   present

C   **For each item, circle the key verb. Then circle the number of actors the verb indicates and circle the tense of the key verb, past or present.**

	Actor(s)	Verb	Other words					
1.		are selling		one	more than one	either	past	present
2.		writes		one	more than one	either	past	present
3.		is chasing		one	more than one	either	past	present
4.		have thought		one	more than one	either	past	present
5.		has been wondering		one	more than one	either	past	present
6.		catches		one	more than one	either	past	present
7.		had been riding		one	more than one	either	past	present
8.		have discovered		one	more than one	either	past	present
9.		bought		one	more than one	either	past	present

Lesson 13

D USE CONSISTENT VERB TENSE

> *Rule:* Key verbs in a passage are usually in the same tense.
> This sentence has a problem:
>   The cranes left here after the weather has turned cold.
> These sentences have the problem fixed:
>   a. The cranes left here after the weather had turned cold.
>   b. The cranes leave here after the weather has turned cold.

Draw a line above the joining word. Circle the subjects. Underline the key verbs. Make the key verbs consistent in tense.

past   1. The birds chirped before the sun comes up.

present 2. Our team could never win until we play good defense.

present 3. He was tired after he walks to school.

past   4. Grandpa has seen a lot of danger when the war ended.

past   5. That child had not yet found the toy before it is bedtime.

END OF LESSON 13

Name _____

14

A USE CONSISTENT VERB TENSE

> You've learned to identify complete sentence parts within a longer sentence. A complete sentence part is called a clause.
>
> A clause is a sentence part that has <u>a subject and a key verb</u>. One sentence can contain one, two, or more clauses.

Draw a line above the joining word in each item. For each clause, circle the subject and underline the key verb. Write the number of complete sentence parts on the line. Then circle the tense past or present.

1. I know why the earth gets warmer after the sun rises. _____

    past   present

2. She wanted to drive when we went to the game. _____

    past   present

3. Her book collection may become larger after the sale. _____

    past   present

4. Rose and Sal were working very hard before the storm. _____

    past   present

5. Those buildings were going up fast until the company ran out of money. _____

    past   present

Lesson 14   33

B Draw a line above the joining word. For each clause, circle the subject and underline the key verb. Cross out the key verb that is wrong and write the correct verb above it.

past   1. Milo studies every night when he was working on his degree.

past   2. He sees the northern lights where he lived twenty years ago.

present   3. They can use a map to figure out where the girls were going.

present   4. We did not want to be bothered with work while we are sailing.

present   5. People can have a good time while they were traveling in Spain.

C For each item, circle the key verb, circle the number of actors, and circle the tense of the key verb.

	Actor(s)	Verb	Other words					
1.		was sleeping		one	more than one	either	past	present
2.		has been hunting		one	more than one	either	past	present
3.		did see		one	more than one	either	past	present
4.		wants		one	more than one	either	past	present
5.		is pushed		one	more than one	either	past	present
6.		have pushed		one	more than one	either	past	present

END OF LESSON 14

Name _____ 15

A USE CONSISTENT VERB TENSE

These words can join two sentences together:
when, where, while, why
before, after, until
although, as, because, if, unless

(The girls) can finish the project if (the teacher) gives them more time. __2__
                 past   (present)

Write the number of clauses in each sentence on the line. Draw a line above the joining word. For each item, circle the subject and underline the key verb. Circle past or present to indicate the tense of the key verbs.

1. Tio felt tired although he did very little. _____

       past   present

2. I can finish the job unless you prefer to do it. _____

       past   present

3. Only one girl knew if the candy was hidden. _____

       past   present

4. She drove the car into the ditch because she had to swerve as an approaching car moved into her lane. _____

       past   present

5. We want to go on a trip after Thanksgiving. _____

       past   present

6. Air becomes less dense as the temperature rises. _____

       past   present

B Write the correct key verb for each blank.

          have   has

1. My sister _____ a new boyfriend.

          have   has

2. The pilot _____ a serious problem.

            have   has

3. Tilly and Bertha _____ bought the same outfits.

      have   has

4. They _____ no idea how to work the problem.

        have   has

5. The largest dog _____ a sore front paw.

          have   has

6. When we go fishing, I _____ a good time.

        have   has

7. Hank and I _____ a bad habit of talking too much.

         have   has

8. Sid, Mel, and Jo _____ more perfect

       have   has

papers than I _____ .

END OF LESSON 15

Name _____   **16**

A Draw a line above the joining word. Circle the subjects. Underline the key verbs. Make the key verbs consistent in tense.

Past   1. Jinah likes to play golf although her clubs were very old.

Past   2. He has refused to write because it could not help to solve the problem.

Present   3. They can bring the dessert if you provided the main dish.

Past   4. He was not going to cash the check unless you have the money to cover it.

Past   5. Many people were riding the train when it crashes.

B USE THE CORRECT VERB FORM

Make subjects agree with regular key verbs in the present tense.

| he, she, it | sees, costs, wishes |
| I, you, they | see, cost, wish |

Circle the correct key verb form.

      have   has

1. That animal _____ a bad smell.

      have   has

2. Those sentences _____ too many words.

      see   sees

3. Doris and Melissa _____ well.

  have   has

4. We _____ asked for the necessary signatures.

  wish   wishes

5. Randy _____ for better weather.

Lesson 16

      have   has

6. Tim and I _____ all the answers right.

      have   has

7. You _____ good instincts.

      cost   costs

8. Jim's house _____ quite a lot.

      have   has

9. Most tables _____ a top and four legs.

      cry   cries

10. The toddler _____ a lot.

C. Circle more general or more specific for each topic.

Title 1: How to Care for Your Dog

1. How to Get Rid of Fleas on Your Dog

    more general   more specific

2. Caring for Pets

    more general   more specific

Title 2: Listening to Music

1. Jazz That Is Easy to Listen To

    more general   more specific

2. Sounds That You Hear

    more general   more specific

3. The Sound of Guitar Music

    more general   more specific

Title 3: Car Repairs Made Easy for Anyone

1. All About Cars

        more general   more specific

2. Replacing Brakes and Mufflers

        more general   more specific

3. Car Repairs for the Beginner

        more general   more specific

END OF LESSON 16

17   Name _____

A   USE THE CORRECT VERB FORM

he, she, it	is
they	are
I	am

Circle the correct key verb form.

        is   are   am

1. Three girls and Tom _____ finishing the assignment.

      have   has

2. Their garden _____ grown more than 4,000 carrots.

  is   are   am

3. I _____ writing a great story.

     is   are   am

4. Marci and she _____ thinking about going to college.

     is   are   am

5. That boat and that cat _____ traveling around the world.

     cost   costs

6. The larger stones _____ more money.

     travel   travels

7. That plane _____ faster than sound.

  has   have

8. He _____ worked as a carpenter.

  have   has

9. We _____ not asked all of our questions yet.

     is   are   am

10. She believes her son _____ marrying a good woman.

B Write the correct key verb in each blank.

        feel   feels   felt   get   gets   got

Present   1. They _____ cold when they _____ out of the water.

        can   could   finish   finishes   finished

Present   2. She _____ watch TV after she _____ her homework.

        freeze   freezes   froze   get   gets   got

Present   3. The lake _____ if it _____ really cold at night.

        love   loves   loved   am   is   are   was   were

Past   4. They _____ to fish in the creek while school _____ out.

END OF LESSON 17

18

A Circle the correct missing word.

have   has

1. Jill _____ completed the assignment.

     run   runs

2. Cheri and Ben _____ five miles every day.

    play   plays

3. That cat _____ all morning.

think   thinks   have   has

4. You _____ you _____ cleaned up the room.

    are   is   am

5. Donna and Bob _____ selling the red car.

buy   buys   travel   travels

6. She _____ earrings every time she _____ .

    have   has

7. They _____ moved to another city.

think   thinks   has   have

8. I _____ Ida _____ watched too much TV.

tell   tells   has   have

9. They _____ me that the horse _____ won 11 races.

    are   is   am

10. Don and Greg _____ absent too much.

Lesson 18

B CONVEY TIMES, SEQUENCES, STATES, AND CONDITIONS

Key verbs in the present tense can refer to events that have not yet happened.

The lion **is going to** attack when it **finds** an antelope.

The lion **may** attack when it **finds** an antelope.

The lion **can** attack when it **finds** an antelope.

All these sentences refer to an event that has not yet happened.

The sentences are in the present tense.

C For each sentence, circle <u>happened</u> if the sentence describes something that happened. Circle <u>not yet</u> if the event has not happened yet.

1. We _____ be having pizza for dinner tonight after everyone _____ come home.

   Happened   Not yet

2. We _____ to have pizza every night last week.

   Happened   Not yet

3. She _____ going to be very angry when she _____ his mistakes.

   Happened   Not yet

4. She _____ going to the ballgame tomorrow as soon as her brother _____ home.

   Happened   Not yet

5. What day _____ the meeting last April?

   Happened   Not yet

6. The store _____ in 1 hour.

   Happened   Not yet

D Classify each item.

1. Riding a bike on a dirt road.

   City   Country   Neither

2. Milking the cow

   City   Country   Neither

Lesson 18   43

3. Eating in restaurants

        City   **Country**   **Neither**

4. Crossing at a traffic light

        City   **Country**   **Neither**

5. Talking on the phone

        City   **Country**   **Neither**

6. Feeding the chickens.

        City   **Country**   **Neither**

7. Riding a rocket to Mars

        City   **Country**   **Neither**

8. Singing in a choir

        City   **Country**   **Neither**

9. Climbing trees in an orchard

        City   **Country**   **Neither**

10. Walking to City Hall

        City   **Country**   **Neither**

11. Parking on the street

        City   **Country**   **Neither**

12. Driving a tractor

        City   **Country**   **Neither**

13. Walking in a park

        City   **Country**   **Neither**

14. Walking to school

        City   **Country**   **Neither**

END OF LESSON 18

Name _____

19

A IDENTIFY CLAUSES IN COMPLEX SENTENCES

> You know that joining words join clauses within sentences.
> Here are the joining words that you've learned:
>
> | when | where | while | why | before | after |
> |------|-------|-------|-----|--------|-------|
> | until | although | as | because | if | unless |

Draw a line over the joining word. Circle the subjects. Underline the key verbs. Write the number of complete sentence parts on the line. Then circle the tense past or present.

1. I may have finished those chores if I do not my homework. ____

   past   present

2. Emilie wants to go fishing without taking her brother along. ____

   past   present

3. She asks her brother if she can ride along after the dance is over. ____

   past   present

4. She asks her brother to drive her to the lake. ____

   past   present

5. He tells her to take the bus on the corner of 10th and Main. ____

   past   present

6. He told her to take the bus after finishing her work. ____

   past   present

7. Monty and Wren asked their mother to go shopping with them. ____

   past   present

Lesson 19   45

B Write the correct key verb in each blank. Make the tense in each sentence consistent.

        plan   plans   planned

Not yet 1. We _____ to have pizza for dinner

        come   comes   came

tonight after everyone _____ home.

        want   wants   wanted

Happened 2. We _____ to have pizza every night last week.

        am   is   are   was   were

Not yet 3. She _____ going to be very angry when she

        see   sees   saw

_____ his mistakes.

        am   is   are   was   were

Not yet 4. She _____ going to the ball game tomorrow

        come   comes   came

as soon as her brother _____ home.

        am   is   are   was   were

Happened 5. What day _____ the meeting last April?

        open   opens   opened

Not Yet 6. The store _____ in one hour.

C **Place commas in these sentences where they are needed.**

1. After Toji gave me a ride to Tintown, we took a detour to Billtown.

2. Without anyone noticing, we set the balloons loose.

3. We will have no time to stop later if you take too long taking pictures now.

4. When Jake finished building the fire, he set up the tent.

5. If you wish, I can pick you up.

6. We set the balloons loose without anyone noticing.

7. If you are willing to work hard, you can make good money.

8. Before taking a break, he finished the side.

END OF LESSON 19

20 Name _____

A IDENTIFY CLAUSES IN COMPLEX SENTENCES

> You know that joining words join clauses within sentences.
> Here are the joining words that you've learned:
>
> | when | where | while | why | before | after |
> |------|-------|-------|-----|--------|-------|
> | until | although | as | because | if | unless |

Draw a line over the joining word. Circle the subjects. Underline the key verbs. Write the number of complete sentence parts on the line. Then circle the tense past or present.

1. That was when she knew why Bobby came home. ____

    past   present

2. He can mow the lawn by himself unless you find another mower. ____

    past   present

3. Dorene is encouraging her mother to join her on the flight to Denver. ____

    past   present

4. Dorene wants to stay in Denver until winter comes. ____

    past   present

5. She loves flying in a plane with flags waving from the tail. ____

    past   present

6. Her mother hated to fly until last year. ____

    past   present

B **Circle each word that is a type of weather.**

Types of Weather

1. morning
2. cloudy
3. sun
4. driving in snow
5. rainy
6. cold
7. thermometer
8. windy
9. foggy
10. stormy
11. rainhat
12. sunny
13. hot

C **Circle the time of each sentence.**

1. After you ▓▓▓ your homework tomorrow, you ▓▓▓ go outside.

    Happened   Not yet

2. The next time you ▓▓▓ your backpack, I ▓▓▓ going to make you pay for a new one.

    Happened   Not yet

3. Last month, Nona ▓▓▓ to her class every day but never ▓▓▓ her friend there once.

    Happened   Not yet

4. We ▓▓▓ walking along Gunson's Ridge last week when we ▓▓▓ the bear and its two cubs.

    Happened   Not yet

5. Lisa ▓▓▓ not watch TV next week unless she ▓▓▓ an A on her test.

    Happened   Not yet

6. Five hours ago I ▓▓▓ how much he ▓▓▓ lift.

    Happened   Not yet

Lesson 20   49

D. Write the correct key verb in each blank.

        finish   finishes   finished

Not yet   1. After you _____ your homework tomorrow,

        can   could

you _____ go outside.

        lose   loses   lost

Not yet   2. The next time you _____ your backpack, I

am   is   are   was   were

_____ going to make you pay for a new one.

        go   goes   went

Happened   3. Last month, Nona _____ to her class every

        see   sees   saw

day, but never _____ her friend there once.

am   is   are   was   were

Happened   4. We _____ walking along Gunson's Ridge

        encounter   encounters   encountered

last week when we _____ the bear and its two cubs.

        can't   couldn't

Not yet   5. Lisa _____ watch TV next week unless she

        get   gets   got

_____ an A on her test.

        see   sees   saw

Happened   6. Five hours ago I _____ how much he

        can   could

_____ lift.

Lesson 20

INDEPENDENT WORK

E **Circle the letter of the statement that is more general.**

Item 1: A. Penguins have feathers.
B. Birds have feathers.

Item 2: A. Mini loves expensive things.
B. Mini loves railroad locomotives.

Item 3: A. Noisy people are annoying.
B. My neighbors are annoying.

Item 4: A. Diamonds were in the collection.
B. Rare stones were in the collection.

F **Place commas in these sentences where they are needed.**

1. Unless it rains tomorrow we are going to the game.

2. When the our home team wins we celebrate.

3. Although Milly has lots of shoes she only wears one pair all the time.

4. While the fish were biting Telio and his friend kept fishing.

5. Until you are out of school you have to follow your parents' rules.

6. The band played until the sun set.

7. After the big storm the place was a mess.

END OF LESSON 20

21

A WRITE AN INFORMATIVE EVENT

Notes

The Human Fly

Breaking News

When: _____

Who: _____

What: _____

Where: _____

Details: _____

_____

_____

_____

Background

born normal
name Igor
playing near Black River, huge bug
sick a month
noticed hands stick
purse lips
walk walls, windows
ceiling

Check N: Did you explain each note?

Check S: Did you include all the words in the notes and spell them correctly?

Check C: Did you put a comma after part of the predicate that is at the beginning of a sentence?

Check T: Did you write a title and underline it?

Check P: Did you write two paragraphs, each with a heading?

■ N   ■ S   ■ C   ■ T   ■ P

INDEPENDENT WORK

B Draw a line over the joining word. Circle the subjects. Underline the key verbs. On the line, write the number of clauses in the sentence. Then circle the tense, <u>past</u> or <u>present</u>.

1. Henry wanted to know why his sister was traveling with his friend. ____   past   present

2. Helen runs with another runner as a pacer. ____   past   present

3. The zebra is staring at the leopard as the leopard creeps through the grass. ____   past   present

4. She knew why the longest line was near the cash register. ____   past   present

5. His argument had many poor sentences because he had not learned how to write well. ____   past   present

C Write the past-tense form.

	Present	Past
1.	see, sees	
2.	catch, catches	
3.	teach, teaches	
4.	lose, loses	
5.	write, writes	
6.	come, comes	
7.	feel, feels	
8.	hear, hears	
9.	know, knows	
10.	stand, stands	

END OF LESSON 21

22 Name _____

A WRITE ABOUT EVENTS

Notes

Dr. Priya Cooper

Recent News

When: _____

Who: _____

What: _____

Where: _____

Details: _____

_____

_____

_____

_____

Background

child no house, no car
aspired, famous researcher
cure common cold
sold to drug company

Check N: Did you explain each note?

Check S: Did you include all the words in the notes and spell them correctly?

Check C: Did you put a comma after part of the predicate that is at the beginning of a sentence?

Check T: Did you write a title and underline it?

Check P: Did you write two paragraphs, each with a heading?

■ N   ■ S   ■ C   ■ T   ■ P

B USE CORRECT VERB TENSE

> You've learned that all key verbs in a passage should usually be in the same tense, past or present.
> The key verb **will** is always used with key verbs in the present tense.
> Here's a sentence that uses the key verb **will**:
>   I **will** see you when you **wave** your hand.
> Remember, use **will** with other present-tense key verbs.

Write the correct key verb to fill in each blank.

                        call   calls   called

Not yet   1. As soon as your parents _____ me, I

         will   would

_____ allow you to get on the bus.

         will   would

Not yet   2. Mia _____ come to see us next week,

         do   does   did

unless she _____ not find a cheap flight.

         finish   finishes   finished

Not yet   3. After you _____ your homework, I

         will   would

_____ help you do the other chores.

         lose   loses   lost

Not yet   4. The next time you _____ your backpack, I

         will   would

_____ make you pay for a new one.

         will   would

Not yet   5. Lisa _____ not be allowed to watch TV next

         get   gets   got

week unless she _____ an A on her test.

Lesson 22

INDEPENDENT WORK

C Draw a line over the joining word. Circle the subjects. Underline the key verbs. On the line, write the number of clauses in the sentence. Then circle the tense, past or present.

1. The girls are discussing the problem as we speak. ____

                                      past   present

2. Bonnie's argument was filled with flaws because she didn't learn the rules. ____

                                      past   present

3. Those butterflies were searching for flowers while the sun was shining. ____

                                      past   present

4. That car is becoming very rusty after all the rain. ____

                                      past   present

5. Her aunt was going to dinner after work. ____

                                      past   present

D Write the present-tense forms of the verbs. One singular verb form ends in s.

	Present	Past
1.		saw
2.		caught
3.		taught
4.		lost
5.		wrote
6.		came
7.		felt
8.		heard
9.		knew
10.		stood

END OF LESSON 22

A Write key verbs in the blanks of each sentence. Make the tenses consistent.

                whistle   whistles   whistled

Happened   1. Tom _____ a cheerful tune as he

                walk   walks   walked

              _____ to school this morning.

                call   calls   called

Not yet   2. As soon as your mother _____ me, I

                will   would

              _____ take you home.

                pay   pays   paid

Happened   3. Last week, Doty _____ her bills but

                forget   forgets   forgot

              _____ to send them.

                is   am   are   was   were

Not yet   4. Rosa _____ coming to see us next

                has   have   had

              week unless she _____ to work.

                find   finds   found

Happened   5. I _____ my keys under the car after I

                back   backs   backed

              _____ out of the driveway.

                start   starts   started

Not yet   6. Class _____ in 10 minutes.

Lesson 23

B USE DIALOG

> Quotes are the exact words that someone says.
>
> **How to Punctuate Quotes**
>
> 1. Capitalize the first word of the sentence and the first word of the direct speech.
>
>   She commented, "You have five minutes."
>   "You have five minutes," she commented.
>
> 2. Place end marks at the end of sentences.
>
>   She commented, "You have five minutes."
>   "You have five minutes," she commented.
>
> 3. Use a comma to separate the direct speech from the words telling who said the direct speech.
>
>   She commented, "You have five minutes."
>   "You have five minutes," she commented.
>
> 4. Place quotation marks around the direct speech. Each quotation mark goes after any other punctuation marks.
>
>   She commented, "You have five minutes."
>   "You have five minutes," she commented.

Punctuate each sentence.

1. she said your bike is nice

2. your bike is nice she said

3. she said there is a better way to do that

4. Bill said I'm 15, but I'll have a birthday next month. I'll be 16

5. I'm 15, but I'll have a birthday next month I'll be 16 Bill said

58   Lesson 23

INDEPENDENT WORK

C Draw a line over the joining word. Circle the subjects. Underline the key verbs. On the line, write the number of clauses in the sentence. Then circle the tense.

1. They were sitting near the stream as it rained. ____

    past   present

2. I know why Andy is in a bad mood today. ____

    past   present

3. Jenny can sing in the show if you play the piano for her. ____

    past   present

4. Our class did a talent show after the first day of spring. ____

    past   present

5. Long programs can be very boring unless they contain a lot of variety. ____

    past   present

D Rewrite each sentence using more familiar language. Don't use the underlined word.

1. The poor girl was cold because she was clad only in light clothing.

   _____

2. Robbers entered her residence.

   _____

3. He aspired to be a great football player.

   _____

4. The estate required 20 people to keep it in order.

   _____

END OF LESSON 23

Lesson 23

24

A USE DIALOG

> Quotes are the exact words that someone says.
>
> **How to Punctuate Quotes**
> 1. Capitalize the first word of the sentence and the first word of the direct speech.
>   He replied, "That's a good idea."
>   "That's a good idea," he replied.
> 2. Place end marks at the end of sentences.
>   He replied, "That's a good idea."
>   "That's a good idea," he replied.
> 3. Use a comma to separate the direct speech from the words telling who said the direct speech.
>   He replied, "That's a good idea."
>   "That's a good idea," he replied.
> 4. Place quotation marks around the direct speech. Each quotation mark goes after any other punctuation marks.
>   He replied, "That's a good idea."
>   "That's a good idea," he replied.

Punctuate each sentence.

1. he called out time is up

2. they need more time she replied

3. he told her you can take another minute

4. you can take another minute he told her

5. he commented that's a better idea let's do it

B IDENTIFY CLAUSES JOINED BY CONJUNCTIONS

Here are joining words that can also be the subject of a clause:
that   who   which   what
1. Her brother bought a car   that was red.
2. She knows   that you are the best.
3. He was looking for the girl   who was sitting on the bench.
4. She can tell you   what comes next.
5. He wants to know   which is best.
6. He wants to know   which horse is best.

Sentence parts that start with **who, which, that,** or **what** are clauses that have key verbs.

C Draw a line above the joining word. Circe the subject of both sentence parts and underline the key verbs.

1. Her brother bought a truck that was blue.

2. She knows who eats cookies.

3. He was looking for the bag that was sitting on the bench.

4. She can tell you what comes next.

5. He wants to know which horse is best.

6. He wants to know which is fastest.

7. She can see that he is a strong swimmer.

END OF LESSON 24

25

A Draw a line above the joining word. Circle the subject and draw a line under the key verb in each clause.

1. She knew what she had to do.

2. He had a difficult time explaining what he thought.

3. Midi has a dog that can eat 3 pounds of dog food in a day.

4. The map will help us figure out which route is best.

5. The fastest runner is the girl who is wearing number 7.

6. He wanted to know who lost his expensive pen.

7. Everyone predicted that we would win the game.

INDEPENDENT WORK

B USE DIALOG

Quotes are the exact words that someone says.

How to Punctuate Quotes
1. Capitalize the first word of the sentence and the first word of the direct speech.
   Her mother said, "Dinner is ready."
   "Dinner is ready," her mother said.
2. Place end marks at the end of sentences.
   Her mother said, "Dinner is ready."
   "Dinner is ready," her mother said.
3. Use a comma to separate the direct speech from the words telling who said the direct speech.
   Her mother said, "Dinner is ready."
   "Dinner is ready," her mother said.
4. Place quotation marks around the direct speech. Each quotation mark goes after any other punctuation marks.
   Her mother said, "Dinner is ready."
   "Dinner is ready," her mother said.

Punctuate each sentence.

1. she said   he lost his kitten

2. I can help you   Tom replied

3. the storm hit us 5 hours ago   he explained

4. Don said   I have a new bike and I love to ride it

C Write the past-tense form of the verb.

	Present	Past
1.	smells	
2.	walks	
3.	studies	
4.	fall	
5.	thinks	
6.	buys	
7.	may	
8.	can	
9.	shall	
10.	do, does	
11.	choose, chooses	
12.	fly, flies	
13.	go, goes	
14.	sit, sits	
15.	run, runs	
16.	sell, sells	
17.	tell, tells	

END OF LESSON 25

26

A CONJUNCTION FUNCTION

You've learned that clauses are complete sentences inside bigger sentences.

You've also used joining words. Joining words that have no other function but to join clauses together are called **conjunctions**.

Here's how you test to see if a word is a conjunction: **If a complete clause follows a word, that word is a conjunction.**
The word **that** is a conjunction in some sentences.

> She argued *that* her brother should help her clean the garage.

The word **that** is not a conjunction in the following sentence: **He bought a car that was red.**

The words **was red** are not a complete clause. So **that** is not a conjunction. **That** is a pronoun. It functions as the subject of the clause, **that was red**.

B For each item, underline the words after the word that. Label the part of speech for that either C for conjunction or P for pronoun. Write KV above the key verbs.

1. He believed that we would win the game.

2. He bought a house that had a large basement.

3. Brown Company is the one that gives the best service.

4. I wish that she had invited me.

5. Ted thought that the meeting was at 1 in the afternoon.

C WRITE INFORMATIVE TEXT

Notes:

<u>Gardening</u>

Green Valley

Where: Florida

        growing season long

When: What:

    February   peas, tomatoes

    March   carrots, cabbage, beans

    beginning in July   great harvest

Blue Valley

Where:

When: What:

Check N: Did you explain each note?

Check S: Did you include all the words in the notes and spell them correctly?

Check C: Did you put a comma after a part of the predicate that is at the beginning of a sentence?

Check T: Did you write a title and underline it?

Check P: Did you write two paragraphs with headings?

◼ N   ◼ S   ◼ C   ◼ T   ◼ P

END OF LESSON 26

27

A USE CORRECT VERB TENSE

Some clauses tell about things that are always true. The key verbs in these clauses are in the **present tense.**

1. Hot air rises.

2. We learned that hot air rises.

3. He always works hard.

4. Ted received an award because he works hard all the time.

5. Ted said that geese fly south every winter.

6. Little Timmy learned that giraffes have long necks.

B Cross out any key verb that is in the wrong tense and write the verb in the correct tense above it.

1. Some students didn't know that 30 x 50 is more than 1300.

2. Yesterday, we learned that the longest days of the year were in June.

3. They found out that the distance from New York to California was more than two thousand miles.

4. The teeter totter did not work because Burt weighed twice as much as Kelly.

5. They were tired because they have worked so hard.

C **Underline the main clause in each sentence. Put a comma in sentences that do not begin with the main clause.**

1. <u>It is an acid</u> if the paper turns red.

2. If the paper turns red, <u>it is an acid</u>.

3. <u>Hana will be happy</u> if she wins the contest.

4. When the album is finished, <u>the machine turns off automatically</u>.

5. <u>Chickens go to their roost</u> when the sun begins to set.

6. When the rooster crows, <u>it is time to get up</u>.

7. <u>Laura told us</u> that shadows get longer as the sun sets.

END OF LESSON 27

A

All the sentences in a paragraph should be on the same topic. Cross out the sentences that do not belong in this paragraph.

TOPIC: Training a Dog

When training a dog, give it clear information about what you want it to do. You do this by telling the dog what to do, then responding to what the dog does. Use simple, one-word commands. ~~Most dogs can sleep inside or outside the house.~~ If the dog follows the command, the trainer should praise it and quickly reward it with a few loving strokes or a treat. ~~Large dogs can eat three or four times as much as small dogs.~~ If the dog does not respond properly, do not reward it. You should never beat the dog. A scolding is enough.

B

Underline the key verbs. One sentence has 3 key verbs. Change the sentence to the past tense.

1. They notice that the squirrel is on their porch.

2. Jane is explaining why the sun sets in the west.

3. My younger brother is learning how hailstones are balls of ice.

4. Our teacher explains that even numbers can be divided by 2.

5. Laura tells us that shadows get longer as the sun goes down.

END OF LESSON 28

Name _____

A CONJUNCTION FUNCTION

> You know how you test to see if a word is a conjunction: **If the words that follow a word make a complete clause, the word is a conjunction.**
>
> Some phrases can function as a conjunction: **She won the race <u>even though</u> she did not run her fastest.**

Draw a line over the conjunctions and underline the key verbs.

1. He has as much as I have.

2. She ran out of gas by the time she had finished half her errands.

3. I will live here as long as I can pay the rent.

4. I bought several flashlights in case we have a power outage.

B Cross out the sentences that do not belong.

TOPIC: Fire Safety

Fire is a wonderful friend, but it is a dangerous enemy. When camping, clear a ten-foot circle around the fire pit. Make sure the circle is cleared of anything that can burn. Flames may be red, yellow, or blue. At home, use a screen to prevent sparks or coals from popping out of the fire. Keep a first-aid kit near your barbecue pit. Barbecued meat tastes better if it is lightly seasoned.

END OF LESSON 29

30

A CONJUNCTION FUNCTION

> You've learned that conjunctions join sentences together.
> The words **and, but,** and **or** are special **conjunctions.** They join any parallel parts together. Here are parallel predicates joined together with the conjunction **and:**
>
> She <u>held a book</u> and <u>drank a cup of tea</u>.
> The boys and girls <u>sang songs</u> and <u>played their ukuleles</u>.
>
> **And, but,** and **or** are called **coordinate conjunctions** because they can join any parallel sentence parts together.

B Underline the parallel parts joined by the conjunctions <u>and</u>, <u>but</u>, <u>or</u>. Write <u>KV</u> over the key verbs.

1. The game started late and finished early.

2. His father talks a lot but does little.

3. My uncle milks cows or drives a tractor.

4. Marla has won many games but has lost even more.

5. Mani and Vio finished their homework and started their other chores.

END OF LESSON 30

31

Name _____

A EXPLAIN IN GENERAL AND IN PARTICULAR

> You've learned that coordinate conjunctions join parallel sentence parts.
>
> a. She was holding a good book and drinking a cup of tea.
>
> > Complete clause for the part after **and:**
> > She was drinking a cup of tea.
>
> To find the parallel parts, cross out the shared words:
> ~~She was~~ holding a good book and drinking a cup of tea.
>
> b. She will sing a song or play the piano.
>
> > Complete clause for the part after **or:**
> > She will play the piano.
>
> ~~She will~~ sing a song or play the piano.

B Cross out the words shared by both clauses. Underline the parallel parts joined by the conjunctions <u>and</u>, <u>but</u>, <u>or</u>. Write <u>KV</u> over the key verbs.

1. She sent emails and texts to her pen pal.

2. The dogs ate bones or puppy chow.

3. She sang and danced with joy.

4. They worked during the day but played in the evening.

5. We have a lot of time but would rather not waste it.

C Cross out the underlined word and write familiar words above it.

1. The Cubs have been playing the Bears for <u>decades</u>.

2. The man <u>set</u> his dog <u>on</u> the raccoon.

3. The <u>incident</u> was reported in the news.

D **Change the sentences to past tense. Cross out any verb that is in the wrong tense and write the verb in the correct tense above it.**

1. They see that the garage door is open.

2. They think that squirrels steal the meat from the garage.

3. I explain to them that squirrels don't eat meat.

4. They discover that the electricity is not working.

INDEPENDENT WORK

E **Draw a line over the joining word. Circle the subjects. Underline the key verbs. On the line, write the number of clauses in the sentence. Then circle the tense.**

1. Our teacher was helping him as he figured out the answer. ____

                        past   present

2. The girls started to laugh when Morris acted silly. ____

                        past   present

3. A large cloud is moving in front of the sun as the temperature drops. ____

                        past   present

4. Our cousins had arrived at the picnic before the storm came in. ____

                        past   present

5. The mice are sneaking around the corners while the cat searches for them. ____

                        past   present

END OF LESSON 31

Name _____

32

A USE CORRECT VERB TENSE

> Some sentences tell you **what to do**.
> **Examples:**
>   Stop at red lights.
>   Look out for falling rocks.
>   Do not talk during the movie.

B Write the passage so it is punctuated properly. Put in capital letters and periods.

exercise every morning work hard in school do not sleep during class listen to your teacher

_____

_____

END OF LESSON 32

33

A Write capitals and periods where they belong.

> you should feed your dog every day take your dog with you to the park throw a ball or a stick dogs love to chase balls

INDEPENDENT WORK

B Draw a line over the joining word. Circle the subjects. Underline the key verbs. On the line, write the number of clauses in the sentence. Then circle the tense.

1. The chairs were heavy although they were made of light metal. ____

    past   present

2. She talks very fast while standing in front of an audience. ____

    past   present

3. The farmer makes money if his crops are good. ____

    past   present

4. Five kittens were tussling in the grass after drinking their mother's milk. ____

    past   present

5. The story did end within five minutes unless my watch stopped working. ____

    past   present

C A student is writing an informational science report for class on the life cycle of fireflies. Read a paragraph from the report and the directions that follow.

> Fireflies lay their eggs in the dirt. Once the eggs hatch underground, the baby fireflies eat and grow. They take about two years to grow into adults and tunnel their way out of the ground. Adult fireflies live for only two or three months.

The student wants to revise the paragraph by adding more information. Circle the number of the one sentence that best supports the topic of the report.

1. Firefly light can be yellow, green, or orange.

2. The baby fireflies, or larvae, eat slugs and worms.

3. Glowworms are related to fireflies, but they cannot fly.

4. I used to live on a farm where there were lots of fireflies.

5. Many animals will not eat fireflies because they have a bitter taste.

END OF LESSON 33

34

A Write capitals and periods where they belong. Underline the key verbs in each sentence.

> everybody should get some form of exercise each day some people hate to exercise that is too bad because exercising helps your body to stay healthy exercise can also be fun if you play games like soccer remember to exercise every day

INDEPENDENT WORK

B Write the conclusion for each argument.

1. All arguments have a conclusion.

   Mary made up an argument.

   _____

2. All row crops grow in Green Valley.

   Corn is a row crop.

   _____

3. On hotter days, water evaporates faster.

   The seventh of July was one of the hotter days.

   _____

4. All types of rare stones were in the collection.

   Diamonds are rare stones.

   _____

5. Bill loves all types of pasta.

   Fettuccini is a type of pasta.

   _____

C Draw a line over any joining words. Circle the subjects. Underline the key verbs. On the line, write the number of clauses in the sentence. Then circle the tense.

1. My uncle is tired because he has been driving a bus all day. ____

    past   present

2. We spent two hours trying to find our way out of the tunnel. ____

    past   present

3. The campers were walking home because they had no car. ____

    past   present

4. Seven dogs had been sniffing the trail while helicopters searched overhead. ____

    past   present

END OF LESSON 34

35 Name _____

A USE COMMA FOR THINGS IN A SERIES

> When you write a sentence that names a series of three or more things, you separate each thing with a comma.
>
> a. The truck was filled with file cabinets, books, and desks.
> b. John, Bonnie, and Clyde went fishing.
> c. Mr. Heffer told his students to be on time, follow directions, and work hard.

Put in commas.

1. She carried a jug of water and a blue towel.

2. They collected rocks driftwood and shells.

3. Swimming biking and hiking are good for your heart.

4. The boys rode their bikes to the field picked strawberries and ate most of them.

5. The students from Hilltown Greenville and Nash had a wonderful track meet.

6. The truck was filled with old newspapers scrap iron and other junk.

B Place commas as needed in these items. Write KV over the key verbs. Write the number of clauses on the line. Circle the tense of the key verbs.

1. We hiked all day and rested all evening. ____

                        past   present

2. We hiked all day and we rested all evening. ____

                        past   present

3. Phil needs to study hard because he wants to pass the test. ____

                        past   present

4. Her feet felt cold and her hands were also cold. ____

                        past   present

5. Snow fell on the hills all day but disappeared quickly. ____

          past   present

6. My mother has to be careful or she will fall. ____

          past   present

7. The horse was stubborn but he always obeyed his master. ____

          past   present

8. He can take it or leave it. ____

          past   present

9. Milo is a great dancer and he knows it well. ____

          past   present

10. Milo is a great dancer and overall a great performer. ____

          past   present

INDEPENDENT WORK

C In each sentence, write a comma if it is needed. Underline the key verbs. Write the number of clauses on the line. Circle the tense of the key verbs, past or present.

1. The weather will get better but that may take a week. ____

          past   present

2. Our new phone will take messages by translating everything into text. ____

          past   present

3. His youngest sister could do magic tricks even though she was not very good ____

          past   present

4. Ted had a lot of money but he would not pay for all the groceries. ____

          past   present

5. The cat ran into the street after Kelly called it. ____

          past   present

D **For each item, figure out the missing evidence to complete the deduction.**

1. _____

    Grapes grown in the Marcell Valley have the best taste.

    Therefore, these grapes have the best taste.

2. _____

    The man hates all dogs.

    Therefore, this man hates Marcie.

3. _____

    Big ships cannot dock in shallow ports.

    Therefore, big ships cannot dock in Newport.

4. _____

    This plate is a thing made of silver.

    Therefore, this plate will tarnish.

END OF LESSON 35

Name _____

36

A Punctuate each sentence properly.

> For dinner she had a salad, chicken, and French fries.

1. Toads have short front legs short back legs and skin that is rough.
2. We found a wheel a screwdriver and an old sign.
3. The closets in the front hall and the living room had been recently painted.
4. I like Andy his father and his youngest brother.
5. She shopped for groceries and gloves.
6. We forgot to bring fresh clothes enough money and sunglasses.

B Complete each table.

jump

	Present	Past
Simple	I jump	_____
Perfect	_____	_____

like

	Present	Past
Simple	He likes cars.	_____
Perfect	_____	_____

END OF LESSON 36

A Make a / to show where a new paragraph starts.

Rule: When a different person talks, you start a new paragraph.

Bill and Sue were riding their bikes on a mountain trail. The riders were going pretty slowly when they came to a steep downhill slope. Sue said, "This hill looks pretty dangerous." "Not really," Bill replied. "We just have to go down without sliding into the ditch." Sue sighed and started her bike down the hill. "Wait!" Bill cried. "Your back tire looks like it's going flat." "Oh no! What are we going to do?" Sue exclaimed.

B Make a / to show where a new paragraph starts.

"Oh no! What are we going to do?" Sue exclaimed. Bill said, "I have an air pump in my pack. We'll pump up the tire and ride until the tire starts to get soft. Then we'll stop and pump it up again." Sue nodded. The riders got off their bikes. Bill pumped up the tire and said, "Let's go downhill." Sue replied, "Yes, but let's go slowly." That's what they did, and they got home safely. When they stopped in front of Sue's house, she said, "Thanks, Bill. I'm sure glad you had a pump." "So am I," Bill replied.

C **Complete each sentence by writing the correct verb.**

1. She walks on a rocky slope.

   Simple past: She _____ on a rocky slope.

   Present perfect: She _____ on a rocky slope.

   Past perfect: She _____ on a rocky slope.

2. He paints expensive bikes.

   Simple past: He _____ expensive bikes.

   Present perfect: He _____ expensive bikes.

   Past perfect: He _____ expensive bikes.

3. They listen to the radio.

   Simple past: They _____ to the radio.

   Present perfect: They _____ to the radio.

   Past perfect: They _____ to the radio.

4. An owl chases a mouse.

   Simple past: An owl _____ a mouse.

   Present perfect: An owl _____ a mouse.

   Past perfect: An owl _____ a mouse.

5. That train climbs a mountain.

   Simple past: That train _____ a mountain.

   Present perfect: That train _____ a mountain.

   Past perfect: That train _____ a mountain.

INDEPENDENT WORK

D **Place commas in the sentences that list 3 or more things.**

1. The best ingredients for salsa are roasted tomatoes sweet onions roasted garlic and roasted peppers.

2. He carried a screwdriver hammer and sharp saw in his tool box.

3. She looked for her purse and keys.

4. My best buddies are Teka my uncle and Josh.

5. We just cleaned the bedroom the family room the kitchen and the bathroom.

6. That car needs new seats headlamps and a bumper.

E **In each sentence, write a comma if needed. Label the key verbs. Draw a line over the conjunction. Write the number of clauses on the line. Circle the tense of the key verbs, past or present.**

1. The day was hot but the wind was strong. ____

   past   present

2. The builders park their trucks on the street or in that lot. ____

   past   present

3. The rain is coming in the window and it makes the floor wet. ____

   past   present

4. The workers are loud but they are doing a super job. ____

   past   present

5. The men are hammering and making a lot of noise. ____

   past   present

6. He finished his homework but he had not cleaned up his room. ____

   past   present

7. His face was sunburned and his nose had blistered. ____

   past   present

END OF LESSON 37

Name _____

A Fill out the table with the verbs.

	Present	Present Perfect	Past	Past Perfect
1.	He works.			
2.	They help.			
3.	We reply.			
4.	She wades.			
5.	You push.			
6.	He calls.			

B USE CORRECT VERB TENSE WITH QUOTATIONS

- Some sentences tell the exact words that somebody said. Those words are in quotes.
- Words in quotes do not change tense no matter what tense the rest of the sentence or passage is.
- Right now, Joe is saying, "My brother will go fishing on Friday."
- Yesterday, Joe said, "My brother will go fishing on Friday."
- Tomorrow, Joe will say, "My brother will go fishing on Friday."
- Remember, the tense of the part of the sentence inside the quotation marks stays the same.

C Fix the passage so it tells about the past. Cross out the wrong verb and write the correct verb above it.

Passage

Tim says, "We will wade across the stream."

Tina complains, "We will get wet."

"We will take our shoes off," Tim replies.

Tim and Tina take off their shoes and wade across.

END OF LESSON 38

Lesson 38

A Fill out the table with just the verbs. Don't write the subject again.

	Present	Present Perfect	Past	Past Perfect
1.	I play.			
2.	They walk.			
3.	We wait.			
4.	He wishes.			
5.	I master.			
6.	They entertain.			

INDEPENDENT WORK

B In each sentence, write a comma if it is needed. Underline the key verbs. Write the number of clauses on the line. Circle the tense of the key verbs, past or present.

1. Her sister was only 8 years old but she looked older. ____

    past   present

2. Our neighbors make noise in the morning and very late at night. ____

    past   present

3. Candy tastes good but I avoid eating too much candy. ____

    past   present

4. We loved to go to the mountains or to a wonderful place on the coast. ____

    past   present

C. Complete each argument.

Argument 1: All animals that do not have a backbone are called invertebrates.
A snail is an animal that does not have a backbone.

_____

Argument 2: As an object in space gets closer to the surface of the earth, the pull of gravity on the object increases.
A spaceship is getting closer to the surface of the earth.

_____

END OF LESSON 39

40

A Fill out the table with just the verbs. Don't write the subject again.

	Present	Present Perfect	Past	Past Perfect
1.	We travel.			
2.	You cry.			
3.	He follows.			
4.	It tilts.			
5.	We design.			
6.	She devours.			

B Write about a pleasant surprise you had.

Sample passage:

<u>My Birthday Surprise</u>

  I had a pleasant surprise on my sixteenth birthday. It was at Julie Becker's place. I thought I was picking her up so we could go to a show together. She said that she would treat me for my birthday.

  When I went inside, about 20 kids jumped out from all over the place. They all shouted, "Surprise!" It was a surprise birthday party, and I didn't have any idea Julie set it up. We had a huge cake with 16 candles for me to blow out.

  After I blew out the candles, I told Julie, "You really surprised me." We had cake, ice cream, and whipped cream.

Check T: Did you write a title and italicize it?

Check P: Did you write several paragraphs?

Check C: Did you use commas correctly?

Check VT: Did you write all the key verbs in the correct tense?

Check Q: Did you use quotes with correct verb tense and paragraphing?

Check EI: Did the passage give **enough information** for the reader to know what happened?

■ T   ■ P   ■ C   ■ VT   ■ Q   ■ EI

C. Change all the keys verbs not in quotes to past tense.

Mona and Dab are crossing a small stream when they almost have a serious accident. "That bridge looks weak," Mona cries.

"Nah, I think it looks fine," Dab says. Then he started across the bridge. Mona follows him. Suddenly, a support on the bridge broke. The bridge tilts to one side.

"Dab, watch out," Mona screamed. She runs to give Dab a hand. Dab grabbed Mona. They both almost fell off the bridge.

"I can grab the rail," Dab said as she reaches for the rail of the bridge. She hung on tight and said to Mona, "Climb over me to the bank."

Mona climbs over Dab and gets to the bank first. Then she said indignantly to Dab, "Dab, I told you that bridge was weak. You better listen to me next time."

END OF LESSON 40

41

Name _____

A WRITE INFORMATIVE ARTICLE

Checks

Check So: Did you name the author of your source?

Check CS: Did you write complete sentences and punctuate them correctly?

Check VT: Did you write all the key verbs in the correct tense?

Check T: Did you write a title and underline it?

Check S: Did you correctly spell all the words in the notes?

☐ So ☐ CS ☐ VT ☐ T ☐ S

B Change this passage to the past tense. Cross out the verb and write the past verb above.

Sam tells me, "Emily will go to France on her vacation." Sam explains that her brother wants to go with her. Sam says that the trip is expensive for them. He says that they are doing odd jobs to make some extra money. "I don't think they can earn enough money to go," Sam claims.

C EXPLAIN IN GENERAL AND IN PARTICULAR

> a. He was washing the car and cleaning the tires.
> b. He sings or plays the piano.
> c. He plays the piano or the flute.

Underline the key verbs in each sentence.

1. They cleaned windows and glass doors on modern homes.

2. We love to sing and dance at parties.

3. We sing and dance at parties.

4. You can be on the team or be the reporter.

5. I love goats but want no more.

6. They have many friends and welcome everyone.

D Fill out the table with just the verbs. Don't write the subject.

	Present	Present Perfect	Past	Past Perfect
1.	They claim.			
2.	I explain.			
3.	He moves.			
4.	She chases.			
5.	We enjoy.			
6.	You work.			

INDEPENDENT WORK

E **Punctuate and capitalize the sentences. Write commas where they are needed.**

Meg is attractive athletic and strong she has been doing strength training almost every day for three years she does three or four sets of each exercise for her warm-up she jumps rope and does 100 sit-ups next she does her main workout she does sets of bench presses squats and curls

F **In each sentence, write a comma if it is needed. Underline the key verbs. Write the number of clauses on the line. Circle the tense of the key verbs, past or present.**

1. She went to the mall and to the train station near the mall. ____

    past   present

2. They love all the food at Tony's but they usually have pizza or Chinese food. ____

    past   present

3. Their car is old and it has a large dent on one side. ____

    past   present

4. Mr. Edison does a lot of complaining but he is nice. ____

    past   present

END OF LESSON 41

Name _____

42

A Fill out the table with just the verbs. Don't write the subject.

	Present	Present Perfect	Past	Past Perfect
1.	They paint.			
2.	Her mother finishes.			
3.	Ron and Gabriel look.			
4.	Tom walks.			
5.	Gina laughs.			
6.	The men snore.			
7.	Joe climbs.			

INDEPENDENT WORK

B In each sentence, write a comma if it is needed. Underline the key verbs. Write the number of clauses on the line. Circle the tense of the key verbs, past or present.

1. Her sister is only 8 years old but she looks older. ____

   past   present

2. Our neighbors make noise in the morning and very late at night. ____

   past   present

3. The candy tasted good and Minni could not stop eating it. ____

   past   present

4. We can go to the mountains or to a wonderful place on the coast. ____

   past   present

END OF LESSON 42

43

Name _____

A Fill in the missing verb forms.

	Present	Past	Perfect
1.	go, goes		
2.	see, sees		
3.	do, does		
4.	give, gives		
5.	know, knows		
6.	take, takes		

B Change this passage to the past tense. Cross out the verb and write the past verb above.

Rachel is very strong because she works on the farm. Carrying heavy things makes her legs strong. Her mother says, "Rachel doesn't mind carrying things. She does not like to clean out the barn." When Rachel tries out for the track team, her coach can not believe how fast she runs. She is the fastest runner on the track team.

INDEPENDENT WORK

C For each item, write a parallel sentence that does not have the word <u>there</u>.

1. There were four dogs in the street.
   _____

2. There is a long line in front of the theater.
   _____

3. There were some large boats on the river.
   _____

4. There are nervous people in the dentist's office.
   _____

END OF LESSON 43

Name _____

A Fill in the missing verb forms.

	Present	Past	Perfect
1.	go, goes		
2.	see, sees		
3.	do, does		
4.	give, gives		
5.	know, knows		
6.	take, takes		

B USE CORRECT VERB TENSE

> You've learned that key verbs in a combined sentence should be in the same tense.
>
> **Exception 1**: Key verbs in clauses that tell something that is always true are in the present tense.
>
> **Exception 2**: Key verbs in quotes keep their tense.

For each item, underline the key verbs. Change key verbs to the past tense as appropriate.

1. The packer works all day, but he was not too tired to go out with friends that night.

2. Ross says, "This is ridiculous."

3. Josh is completing his homework, and then he can visit his father.

4. Horace fed the sheep, or he waters the horses.

5. She wants to cry, but nobody knew her pain.

Lesson 44

C Write the answer to each question and check the box to indicate the source.

Source 1

On Monday morning, Ms. Hassel returned English and math tests to her class and explained her grading system.

Here's a summary: One hundred points were possible.

Fifty points were possible on the math test.

Fifty points were possible on the English test.

Each test required students to earn at least 30 points.

A student needed a total score of 70 points to pass the test.

Two students did not pass the English test.

All students passed the math test.

The hardest part was the editing part of the English test. Many students left words misspelled, and the students were weak on placing commas appropriately.

Students who did well all year on the homework assignments did well on the tests.

Two students who did little or no homework also did well on the tests.

The two students who scored less than 30 on the English test will spend some extra time with the teacher this week. They will take the test again on Friday.

Source 2

Student	Math	English	Total	Absent
1. Alvin	36	48	84	
2. Owen	42	29	71	
3. Kim	50	35	85	
4. Frank				x
5. Sharon	46	45	91	
6. Rainbow	41	39	80	
7. Tofu	37	33	70	
8. Henry	49	47	96	
9. Joseph	33	24	57	
10. Brian	46	42	88	
11. Cecily				x
12. Marilyn	44	41	85	
13. Laurie	48	45	93	
14. James	50	49	99	
15. Peter	41	43	84	
16. Martha	39	37	76	
17. Nancy	43	39	82	
18. David	46	41	87	
19. Leroy	37	39	76	
20. Candice	41	42	83	
21. Mary	50	49	99	
22. Nickolas	48	42	90	
23. Mick	39	34	73	
24. Tina	49	38	77	
25. Regina	45	40	75	

Questions

Check the boxes to match each source with the idea or ideas that it supports. Some ideas may have more than one source. Some ideas may have no source.

	Source 1	Source 2	Neither
1. How many points are possible on the entire test? _____	☐	☐	☐
2. Does the English test or the math test have the higher possible score? _____	☐	☐	☐
3. Did more students pass the English part of the test or the math part? _____	☐	☐	☐
4. What are the last names of the two students who scored lower than 30 on the English test? _____	☐	☐	☐
5. How many students took the test? _____	☐	☐	☐
6. How many students were absent? _____	☐	☐	☐
7. How many students scored less than 30 on the English part of the test? _____	☐	☐	☐

END OF LESSON 44

Lesson 44

45

Name _____

A FORM AND USE THE PERFECT TENSE

Irregular verb — know

	Present	Past
Simple	know, knows	knew
perfect	has known	had known
	have known	

B Fill in the missing verb forms.

	Present	Past	Perfect
1.	go, goes		
2.	see, sees		
3.	do, does		
4.	give, gives		
5.	know, knows		
6.	take, takes		

C Change this passage to the past tense. Cross out the verb and write the past-tense verb above.

My mother wants to remodel the kitchen. She feels that she does not have enough counter space. My dad keeps telling her, "We do not have enough money to make all the changes that you want." She points out that it will not cost too much if my sister and I do most of the work. I have told her, "We don't know how to do countertops. But we can paint the walls."

D **Underline the key verbs. Change them to the past tense as appropriate.**

1. The weather is getting better, but that had been a long time coming.

2. Our new phone took messages, and it translates everything into text.

3. His youngest sister is doing magic tricks, but she was not very good.

4. Ted agreed to the plan, and he pays for all the groceries.

5. The cat runs into the street, but Kelly did not follow it.

E **USE SOURCES**

Questions

Check the boxes to match each source with the idea or ideas that it supports. Some ideas may have more than one source. Some ideas may have no source.

	Source 1	Source 2	Neither
1. Name one thing you can do to prevent frostbite.	☐	☐	☐
2. How long before frostbite may heal?	☐	☐	☐
3. How long before the doctor knows whether to amputate or not?	☐	☐	☐
4. How many people get frostbite in one year?	☐	☐	☐
5. Which is warmer—mittens or gloves?	☐	☐	☐
6. What does frostbite look like?	☐	☐	☐
7. What should you consider when deciding whether to wear extra socks?	☐	☐	☐

END OF LESSON 45

A Write the answer to each question and check the box to indicate the source.

Questions

Check the boxes to match each source with the idea or ideas that it supports. Some ideas may have more than one source. Some ideas may have no source.

	Source 1	Source 2	Both
1. On what day of the week did the river first go above flood level? _____	☐	☐	☐
2. Where did the flooding begin? _____	☐	☐	☐
3. How many feet above normal is the flood level? _____	☐	☐	☐
4. What is the name of the river? _____	☐	☐	☐
5. How many days after the rain stopped did the people return to their homes? _____	☐	☐	☐

B Fill in the missing verb forms.

	Present	Past	Perfect
1.	throw, throws		
2.	write, writes		
3.	drive, drives		
4.	ride, rides		
5.	fly, flies		
6.	eat, eats		

C **Underline key verbs. Make all the key verbs past tense.**

1. Her feet felt cold, and her hands were also cold.

2. Snow fell on the hills all day, but the snow disappears quickly.

3. My mother has to be careful, so she did not fall.

4. Josh is running every day to prepare for the track meet, and his brother timed every one of his runs.

5. The shortest path went under the bridge, but it took a long time to go that way.

INDEPENDENT WORK

D **Fill in the missing verb forms.**

	Present	Past	Perfect
1.	go, goes		
2.	see, sees		
3.	do, does		
4.	give, gives		
5.	know, knows		
6.	take, takes		

E **Rewrite each sentence so it is completely parallel. Punctuate the sentence correctly.**

1. The dog was energetic but irritating.
   _____

2. Martha had a sore leg and a bruised ankle.
   _____

3. My sister will quit her job or go insane.
   _____

F **For each item, write a parallel sentence that does not have the word there. Circle the subject and underline the key verb.**

1. There are four climbers on the side of that mountain.
   _____

2. There was a young girl who lived in the town of Freedom.
   _____

3. There were six dogs trying to catch a squirrel.
   _____

END OF LESSON 46

Name _____

A Fill in the missing verb forms.

	Present	Past	Perfect
1.	throw, throws		
2.	write, writes		
3.	drive, drives		
4.	ride, rides		
5.	fly, flies		
6.	eat, eats		

END OF LESSON 47

48

A Fill in the missing verb forms.

	Present	Past	Perfect
1.	throw, throws		
2.	write, writes		
3.	drive, drives		
4.	ride, rides		
5.	fly, flies		
6.	eat, eats		

END OF LESSON 48

Name _____

49

A RULE FOR COMMA IN COMBINED SENTENCES

Comma Rules

When you write a sentence that names a series of three or more things, you separate each thing with a comma.

If the part after **or, and, but** is a sentence, you place a comma before the joining word.

A. My sister will go hiking, swimming, or shopping.
B. My sister will go swimming, or she will go shopping.
C. My sister will go swimming or go shopping.

B Place commas where they are needed.

1. He washed the car waxed it and drove it around town.

2. Her sister worked at the bakery and at the donut factory.

3. He rode around town and he waved to his friends.

4. She finished her math homework and she talked to her science teacher.

5. She wanted to buy bread eggs and shoelaces.

6. The eggs fell on the floor and made a mess.

7. The cat ran into the street and Kelly yelled at it.

8. Our new phone can take messages and it understands the things we tell it to do.

9. This book tells about gas engines steam engines and how they work.

C KEY VERBS AND CONTRACTIONS

Sometimes key verbs are part of a contraction.

1. I'm happy.   I am happy.
2. We don't want to go.   We do not want to go.
3. He doesn't remember.   He does not remember.

D Change these sentences to the past tense.

1. I'm beginning to like spinach, but I still don't like broccoli.

2. We have taken the wrong road, so we decide to stay overnight.

3. You have noticed the new paint job, and that makes me happy.

4. Joe has met my uncle, but he doesn't remember.

5. Everything possible has been done, but the faucet continues to leak.

6. The story has been reported on the radio, but no one is listening.

7. Meg has been to the county fair, and she is not going again.

END OF LESSON 49

Name _____

A Fill in the missing verb forms.

Verb Forms

	Present	Past	Perfect
1.	is, am, are		
2.	choose, chooses		
3.	begin, begins		
4.	become, becomes		
5.	break, breaks		
6.	drink, drinks		
7.	think, thinks		
8.	buy, buys		

B Place commas where they are needed.

1. Jan likes cookies so much.

2. We brought chairs so we could sit in the shade.

3. I don't like to ride with Mitch so I am walking.

4. I don't want to go where there are no waves and sit on my surfboard.

5. Most dogs sleep well inside or outside the house.

6. The weather will get better but that may take a week.

7. We looked at the sun the clouds and the color of the sky.

8. The longest boat had a cabin and a large deck.

9. I had to ride on a plane an old bus and a really old car.

10. His youngest sister could do magic tricks so she was always invited to parties.

11. Ted agreed with the plan and he told us he would pay for all the groceries.

C **Edit these sentences so that all the key verbs are in the past tense.**

1. Marla tells a good story and then later changed the ending.

2. They searched for gold for years but finally give up.

3. The mice made nests in cars and caused a lot more trouble.

4. Jan looked out the back window and steps on the gas.

5. A boy arrives with the announcement and gives it to a teacher.

6. She sang a beautiful song and plays the piano.

INDEPENDENT WORK

D **Fill in the missing verb forms.**

	Present	Past	Perfect
1.	go, goes		
2.	see, sees		
3.	do, does		
4.	give, gives		
5.	know, knows		
6.	take, takes		
7.	throw, throws		
8.	write, writes		
9.	drive, drives		
10.	ride, rides		
11.	fly, flies		
12.	eat, eats		

E For each statement that makes the Balder Inn look good, write G. For each statement that makes the Balder Inn look bad, write B.

1. The Balder Inn is on the beach. ____

2. The Balder Inn is one of the most beautiful hotels in the United States. ____

3. There are a lot of rats and cockroaches in the Balder Inn. ____

4. All the rooms have TVs. ____

5. The TVs in the Balder Inn do not have cable and pick up only three channels. ____

6. All rooms have large bathrooms with a shower, tub, and marble counters. ____

7. The Balder Inn attracts a large number of tourists. ____

8. Very few tourists visit the Balder Inn more than once. ____

9. There is only hot water from midnight to 7 a.m. in the morning. ____

10. The rooms with fireplaces cost $800 a night. ____

END OF LESSON 50

51

A Edit these sentences so that all the key verbs are in the past tense.

1. Josh is bringing over his new truck and is giving rides.

2. Josh is bringing over his new truck and giving rides.

3. Marge is finishing her homework and turning it in.

4. They are fishing in the lake and hiking in the woods.

5. She has been to the theater and has seen the movie.

B FORM AND USE THE PERFECT TENSE

Irregular verb — choose

	Present	Past
Simple	choose, chooses	chose
Perfect	has chosen have chosen	had chosen

C Fill in the missing verb forms.

	Present	Past	Perfect
1.	is, am, are		
2.	choose, chooses		
3.	begin, begins		
4.	become, becomes		
5.	break, breaks		
6.	drink, drinks		
7.	think, thinks		
8.	buy, buys		

END OF LESSON 51

Name _____ 52

A Edit these sentences so every key verb is in the past tense.

1. John goes to the County fair, but he was not going again.

2. The goats ate all morning and sleep all afternoon.

3. We have seen the movie before, so we decide not to go along.

4. The story is reported on the radio but nobody listened.

5. She is singing and playing the piano.

6. The group makes plans and argued.

B FORM AND USE THE PERFECT TENSE

Irregular verb — begin

	Present	Past
Simple	begin, begins	began
Perfect	has begun have begun	had begun

C Fill in the missing verb forms.

	Present	Past	Perfect
1.	is, am, are		
2.	choose, chooses		
3.	begin, begins		
4.	become, becomes		
5.	break, breaks		
6.	drink, drinks		
7.	think, thinks		
8.	buy, buys		

END OF LESSON 52

53

Name _____

A Fill in the missing verb forms.

Verb Forms

	Present	Past	Perfect
1.	has, have		
2.	ring, rings		
3.	sing, sings		
4.	swing, swings		
5.	sting, stings		
6.	tear, tears		
7.	swear, swears		
8.	bite, bites		
9.	freeze, freezes		

B DETERERMINE THE MEANING OF WORDS

> **Passage 1**
> The ocean was really rough. In contrast, a nearby lake was always **placid**.

1. What part of speech is **placid**? _____

2. What does **placid** probably mean? _____

3. What other information in the passage helped you figure out what **placid** probably means? _____

Stop

4. According to the dictionary, what does the adjective **placid** mean? _____

Passage 2
> He didn't know the exact number of people, but he **estimated** that there were about 200 people.

1. What part of speech is **estimated**? _____

2. What does **estimated** probably mean? _____
   _____

3. What other information in the passage helped you figure out what **estimated** probably means? _____
   _____

Stop

4. According to the dictionary, what does the verb **estimate** mean?
   _____

C Place commas where they are needed.

1. The bicycle skidded on the wet road went into the ditch and hit a rock.

2. I have no money so I need to get a job.

3. Her father gave her his favorite book and told her to read it.

4. Ted carried all the boxes and Henna carried all the papers.

5. The paper flew out of the car window landed near the curb and got soaked.

6. My idea is the best one and everybody acknowledges that.

Lesson 53

INDEPENDENT WORK

D **Rewrite this passage fixing all the errors. Each sentence has one error.**

They opened a new mall. We went there with Jerry his mother laughed the whole time. There were lots of clowns who gave away balloons. Jerry thought that we have too many balloons. We are getting dizzy from blowing them up. One balloon kept losing it's air.

_____

_____

_____

E **Fill in the table with the correct verbs.**

	Present	Past	Perfect
1.	go, goes		
2.	see, sees		
3.	do, does		
4.	give, gives		
5.	know, knows		
6.	take, takes		
7.	throw, throws		
8.	write, writes		
9.	drive, drives		
10.	ride, rides		

	Present	Past	Perfect
11.	fly, flies		
12.	eat, eats		
13.	is, am, are		
14.	choose, chooses		
15.	begin, begins		
16.	become, becomes		
17.	break, breaks		
18.	drink, drinks		
19.	think, thinks		
20.	buy, buys		

END OF LESSON 53

Name _____

54

A Replace the underlined word or words with a new vocabulary word, <u>estimate</u> or <u>placid</u>. Write the new word on the line after each sentence.

1. Several reports <u>guessed</u> that repairing the bridge would cost 2 million dollars.

2. The bay was not as <u>calm</u> as they said it would be.

3. We have to <u>calculate approximately</u> how much of the valley will be destroyed.

B FORM AND USE THE PERFECT TENSE

Irregular verb — ring

	Present	Past
Simple	ring, rings	rang
Perfect	has rung have rung	had rung

C Fill in the missing verb forms.

Verb Forms

	Present	Past	Perfect
1.	has, have		
2.	ring, rings		
3.	sing, sings		
4.	swing, swings		
5.	sting, stings		
6.	tear, tears		
7.	swear, swears		
8.	bite, bites		
9.	freeze, freezes		

Lesson 54   115

INDEPENDENT WORK

D **Make all the key verbs past tense.**

1. Josh wants a new backpack after he finishes his big hike.

2. We take the wrong road after we have argued so long over the map.

3. We buy popcorn after the movie.

4. He smiles when his part was over.

5. I drop my plate when the thunder roars.

6. On Saturday, MaySun waits until the janitor leaves.

7. Last March, the tulips bloom before the snow falls.

E **Rewrite each sentence so it has a silly meaning.**

1. The rabbit ate more than three mice ate.

2. The rabbit ate more than 36 grams of fat.

3. Bees like nectar as much as flies do.

4. John loved the new truck much more than his wife did.

5. Ellen purchased more than her friend Janice purchased.

F Fill in the table with the correct verbs.

	Present	Past	Perfect
1.	go, goes		
2.	see, sees		
3.	do, does		
4.	give, gives		
5.	know, knows		
6.	take, takes		
7.	throw, throws		
8.	write, writes		
9.	drive, drives		
10.	ride, rides		

	Present	Past	Perfect
11.	fly, flies		
12.	eat, eats		
13.	is, am, are		
14.	choose, chooses		
15.	begin, begins		
16.	become, becomes		
17.	break, breaks		
18.	drink, drinks		
19.	think, thinks		
20.	buy, buys		

END OF LESSON 54

55

Name _____

A Place commas where they are needed.

1. The plane left the gate rolled to the runway and roared into the sky.

2. He put in all of the chocolates and cooked the mixture for 12 minutes.

3. She decided to go shopping buy four tools and repair the porch.

4. Four books and seven magazines were on the shelf.

5. The best meat comes from Texas so I only buy meat from Texas.

6. The black tube was six feet long and the other tube fit inside it.

B FORM AND USE THE PERFECT TENSE

Irregular verb — sing

	Present	Past
Simple	sing, sings	sang
Perfect	has sung have sung	had sung

C Fill in the missing verb forms.

Verb Forms

	Present	Past	Perfect
1.	has, have		
2.	ring, rings		
3.	sing, sings		
4.	swing, swings		
5.	sting, stings		
6.	tear, tears		
7.	swear, swears		
8.	bite, bites		
9.	freeze, freezes		

INDEPENDENT WORK

D **Make all the key verbs past tense.**

1. Marge states why she is eating nutritious foods.

2. I know why the fish are not biting.

3. Logan knows where the plane lands in Tintown.

4. Walker states why the argument is contradictory.

5. She knows how to find the hidden cave.

6. The Keystone Library is a place where many people borrow books.

7. That is the house where people play video games.

8. They are telling us why they have moved away.

E **Fill in the table with the correct verbs.**

	Present	Past	Perfect
1.	go		
2.	see		
3.	do		
4.	give		
5.	know		
6.	take		
7.	throw		
8.	write		
9.	drive		
10.	ride		

	Present	Past	Perfect
11.	fly		
12.	eat		
13.	is, am, are		
14.	choose		
15.	begin		
16.	become		
17.	break		
18.	drink		
19.	think		
20.	buy		

END OF LESSON 55

56

Name _____

A Fill in the missing verb forms.

Verb Forms

	Present	Past	Perfect
1.	bring, brings		
2.	come, comes		
3.	feel, feels		
4.	find, finds		
5.	forget, forgets		
6.	get, gets		
7.	hear, hears		
8.	make, makes		
9.	take, takes		

B Read the passage. Use <u>context</u> to figure out what the boldface word means and answer the questions.

> *Passage*
> He looked like a gentle old man, but he has done some **nefarious** things. He stole money from his club. He cheated in the card game. He forged someone else's signature on a legal document.

Questions

1. What part of speech is **nefarious**? _____

2. What does **nefarious** probably mean? _____
_____

3. What other information in the passage helped you figure out what **nefarious** probably means? _____

Stop

4. According to the dictionary, what does **nefarious** mean?
_____

Lesson 56

C Rewrite each sentence with an interesting adjective before the noun.

1. He likes dogs.
   _____

2. She has hair.
   _____

3. We went to a game.
   _____

INDEPENDENT WORK

D Make all the key verbs past tense.

1. Sidney stops working after he hears the bell ring.

2. The woman owns four cars although only one has been paid for.

3. That is when he goes to France to study.

4. This drawer is where I keep my t-shirts.

5. Because her teeth are chattering, Linda clenches her jaw.

6. He burns his nose as he blows out the candles on the cake.

7. Miquel knows that his running time is too slow to win.

E Fill each table with the correct verbs.

	Present	Past	Perfect
1.	go, goes		
2.	see, sees		
3.	do, does		
4.	give, gives		
5.	know, knows		
6.	take, takes		
7.	throw, throws		
8.	write, writes		
9.	drive, drives		
10.	ride, rides		
11.	fly, flies		
12.	eat, eats		
13.	is, am, are		
14.	choose, chooses		
15.	begin, begins		

	Present	Past	Perfect
16.	become, becomes		
17.	break, breaks		
18.	drink, drinks		
19.	think, thinks		
20.	buy, buys		
21.	has, have		
22.	ring, rings		
23.	sing, sings		
24.	swing, swings		
25.	sting, stings		
26.	tear, tears		
27.	swear, swears		
28.	bite, bites		
29.	freeze, freezes		

END OF LESSON 56

A

Replace the underlined word or words with a new vocabulary word. Write the new vocabulary word above the underlined word in each sentence.

Word list: estimate   placid   nefarious

1. They spent time trying to guess how much the repairs would cost.

2. People said that she was an evil person.

3. The water was not as calm as it had been last week.

4. I can't guess how tall that building is.

B   FORM AND USE PERFECT TENSE

Irregular verb — come

	Present	Past
Simple	come, comes	came
Perfect	have come has come	had come

C   Fill in the missing verb forms.

Verb Forms

Present	Past	Perfect
1. bring, brings		
2. come, comes		
3. feel, feels		
4. find, finds		
5. forget, forgets		
6. get, gets		
7. hear, hears		
8. make, makes		
9. take, takes		

Lesson 57

INDEPENDENT WORK

D **Rewrite each sentence with an interesting adjective before the noun.**

1. We have bicycles.
   _____

2. They cleaned the shed.
   _____

3. We saw a bird.
   _____

E **Rewrite each sentence that has a silly meaning.**

1. The bulldozer tore down more than the tractor.
   _____

2. Quincy built more than his brother.
   _____

3. My sister loves cookies more than cake.
   _____

4. She liked the book more than Darlene.
   _____

F. Fill each table with the correct verbs.

	Present	Past	Perfect
1.	go, goes		
2.	see, sees		
3.	do, does		
4.	give, gives		
5.	know, knows		
6.	take, takes		
7.	throw, throws		
8.	write, writes		
9.	drive, drives		
10.	ride, rides		
11.	fly, flies		
12.	eat, eats		
13.	is, am, are		
14.	choose, chooses		
15.	begin, begins		

	Present	Past	Perfect
16.	become, becomes		
17.	break, breaks		
18.	drink, drinks		
19.	think, thinks		
20.	buy, buys		
21.	has, have		
22.	ring, rings		
23.	sing, sings		
24.	swing, swings		
25.	sting, stings		
26.	tear, tears		
27.	swear, swears		
28.	bite, bites		
29.	freeze, freezes		

END OF LESSON 57

58   Name _____

A Write the vocabulary word that has the same meaning above the underlined word in each sentence.

> *Word list:*   estimate   placid   nefarious

1. I could not <u>guess</u> how many people were at the beach on Sunday.

2. He was considered a dangerous person, but not as <u>evil</u> as his brother.

B **FORM AND USE PERFECT TENSE**

Irregular verb — feel

	Present	Past
Simple	feel, feels	felt
Perfect	have felt has felt	had felt

C Fill in the missing verb forms.

Verb Forms

	Present	Past	Perfect
1.	bring, brings		
2.	come, comes		
3.	feel, feels		
4.	find, finds		
5.	forget, forgets		
6.	get, gets		
7.	hear, hears		
8.	make, makes		
9.	take, takes		

INDEPENDENT WORK

D Rewrite each sentence with an interesting adjective before the noun.

1. He has cats.
   _____

2. They stopped at a house.
   _____

3. He carried a load.
   _____

E Fill each table with the correct verbs.

	Present	Past	Perfect
1.	go, goes		
2.	see, sees		
3.	do, does		
4.	give, gives		
5.	know, knows		
6.	take, takes		
7.	throw, throws		
8.	write, writes		
9.	drive, drives		
10.	ride, rides		
11.	fly, flies		
12.	eat, eats		
13.	is, am, are		
14.	choose, chooses		
15.	begin, begins		

	Present	Past	Perfect
16.	become, becomes		
17.	break, breaks		
18.	drink, drinks		
19.	think, thinks		
20.	buy, buys		
21.	has, have		
22.	ring, rings		
23.	sing, sings		
24.	swing, swings		
25.	sting, stings		
26.	tear, tears		
27.	swear, swears		
28.	bite, bites		
29.	freeze, freezes		

END OF LESSON 58

59 Name _____

A Read the passage. Use context to figure out what the boldface word means and answer the questions.

> **Passage**
> The Internet was not used much at first. Now, the Internet is **ubiquitous**.

Questions

1. What part of speech is **ubiquitous**? _____

2. What does **ubiquitous** probably mean? _____
   _____

3. What other information in the passage helped you figure out what **ubiquitous** probably means? _____
   _____

Stop

4. According to the dictionary, what does **ubiquitous** mean?
   _____

B FORM AND USE PERFECT TENSE

Irregular verb — find

	Present	Past
Simple	find, finds	found
Perfect	have found has found	had found

128   Lesson 59

C. Fill in the missing verb forms.

Verb Forms

	Present	Past	Perfect
1.	bring, brings		
2.	come, comes		
3.	feel, feels		
4.	find, finds		
5.	forget, forgets		
6.	get, gets		
7.	hear, hears		
8.	make, makes		
9.	take, takes		

Verb Forms

	Present	Past	Perfect
10.	is, am, are		
11.	choose, chooses		
12.	begin, begins		
13.	become, becomes		
14.	break, breaks		
15.	drink, drinks		
16.	think, thinks		
17.	buy, buys		

END OF LESSON 59

60

A Write a new vocabulary word above an underlined word with the same meaning.

Word list: ubiquitous   estimate   placid   nefarious

1. The birds seemed to be everywhere.

2. The brothers had a reputation for being evil.

3. Harry didn't know how to make a good guess of the cost.

4. The ocean was calm.

END OF LESSON 60

Name _____

61

A DETERMINE THE MEANING OF WORDS

> *Passage 1*
> The boys tried to **extricate** themselves from the crawl space under the house. But they were stuck.

1. What part of speech is **extricate**? _____

2. What does **extricate** probably mean? _____
   _____

3. What information in the passage helped you figure out what **extricate** probably means? _____
   _____

Stop

4. According to the dictionary, what does **extricate** mean?
   _____

> *Passage 2*
> It rained during most of the morning. The sky was very dark, and some of the clouds looked almost black. Then the clouds began to **dissipate,** and the sun came out.

1. What part of speech is **dissipate**? _____

2. What does **dissipate** probably mean? _____
   _____

3. What information in the passage helped you figure out what **dissipate** probably means? _____
   _____

Stop

4. According to the dictionary, what does the **dissipate** mean?
   _____

Lesson 61

B FORM AND USE PERFECT TENSE

Irregular verb — forget

	Present	Past
Simple	forget, forgets	forgot
Perfect	has forgotten have forgotten	had forgotten

C Fill in the missing verb forms.

Verb Forms

	Present	Past	Perfect
1.	bring, brings		
2.	come, comes		
3.	feel, feels		
4.	find, finds		
5.	forget, forgets		
6.	get, gets		
7.	hear, hears		
8.	make, makes		
9.	take, takes		

Verb Forms

	Present	Past	Perfect
10.	have, has		
11.	ring, rings		
12.	sing, sings		
13.	swing, swings		
14.	sting, stings		
15.	tear, tears		
16.	swear, swears		
17.	bite, bites		
18.	freeze, freezes		

END OF LESSON 61

Name _____

A Fill in the missing verb forms.

Verb Forms

	Present	Past	Perfect
1.	pay, pays		
2.	say, says		
3.	run, runs		
4.	put, puts		
5.	sell, sells		
6.	tell, tells		
7.	sit, sits		
8.	sleep, sleeps		
9.	speak, speaks		

INDEPENDENT WORK

B Fill in the missing verb forms.

	Present	Past	Perfect
1.	go, goes		
2.	see, sees		
3.	do, does		
4.	give, gives		
5.	know, knows		
6.	take, takes		
7.	throw, throws		
8.	write, writes		
9.	drive, drives		
10.	ride, rides		

	Present	Past	Perfect
11.	fly, flies		
12.	eat, eats		
13.	is, am, are		
14.	choose, chooses		
15.	begin, begins		
16.	become, becomes		
17.	break, breaks		
18.	drink, drinks		
19.	think, thinks		
20.	buy, buys		

C Write a new vocabulary word above each underlined word that means the same.

Word list: ubiquitous   estimate   nefarious
placid   dissipate   extricate

1. There were so many marbles on the floor Heidi had trouble <u>guessing</u> how many there were.

2. It was a very difficult wrestling match. Both wrestlers were quick and very good at taking advantage of any mistake the other wrestler made. They were also good at <u>freeing</u> themselves from good holds.

3. He looked like a shy librarian, but he was a very <u>evil</u> person.

4. This time of year the flowers in the park are <u>everywhere</u>.

5. George <u>scattered</u> his fortune buying the most expensive home, car, boats, and other luxury items. In the end, he had no money left.

END OF LESSON 62

Name _____

A FORM AND USE PERFECT TENSE

Irregular verb — run

	Present	Past
Simple	run, runs	ran
Perfect	has run have run	had run

B Fill in the missing verb forms.

Verb Forms

	Present	Past	Perfect
1.	pay, pays		
2.	say, says		
3.	run, runs		
4.	put, puts		
5.	sell, sells		
6.	tell, tells		
7.	sit, sits		
8.	sleep, sleeps		
9.	speak, speaks		

INDEPENDENT WORK

C Fill in the missing verb forms.

Verb Forms

Present	Past	Perfect
1. bring, brings		
2. come, comes		
3. feel, feels		
4. find, finds		
5. forget, forgets		
6. get, gets		
7. hear, hears		
8. make, makes		
9. take, takes		

Verb Forms

Present	Past	Perfect
10. have, has		
11. ring, rings		
12. sing, sings		
13. swing, swings		
14. sting, stings		
15. tear, tears		
16. swear, swears		
17. bite, bites		
18. freeze, freezes		

D Write a new vocabulary word above each underlined word that means the same.

Word list: ubiquitous   nefarious   placid
dissipate   extricate

1. Even though the crowd was angry, he remained very calm.

2. The group of boys coming down the street looked evil.

3. The pool chemical spreads in the water.

4. The advertisements on TV were so abundant, we could hardly watch our show.

END OF LESSON 63

A DETERMINE THE MEANING OF WORDS

Passage

Greg told his brother Mark about the new game they played after school. The name of the game was rugby. "It's a lot of fun, hitting other guys, rolling around in the mud. I love it."

Mark decided to go with his brother for the next rugby practice. He thought it would be fun, but it was a **melee** with people tackling him, throwing him down, sitting on his head, and yelling. Mark left the practice with a torn shirt, shoes that looked like mud pies, and a black eye. That was the last rugby practice for Mark.

1. What part of speech is **melee**? _____

2. What does **melee** probably mean? _____
_____

3. What information in the passage helped you figure out what **melee** probably means? _____
_____

Stop

4. According to the dictionary, what does **melee** mean?
_____

Lesson 64 137

B Write the verb in the indicated tense.

1. She told her story.

   Past-perfect: She _____ her story.

2. The women had slept all night.

   Simple past: The women _____ all night.

3. Tom and Jamie paid a bag of food.

   Present-perfect: Tom and Jamie _____ for a bag of food.

4. Both cars traveled too fast for the road conditions.

   Past-perfect: Both cars _____ too fast for the road conditions.

5. Most chickens eat seeds.

   Present-perfect: Most chickens _____ seeds.

6. Regina sells vegetables from her garden next to the house.

   Present-perfect: Regina _____ vegetables from her garden next to the house.

7. He said so much that I got bored.

   Past-perfect: He _____ so much that I got bored.

8. He put his luggage in the closet.

   Present-present: He _____ his luggage in the closet.

9. Kayla and her sister sit on the couch.

   Past-perfect: Kayla and her sister _____ on the couch.

10. Four mice run around the room.

    Present-perfect: Four mice _____ each other around the room.

INDEPENDENT WORK

C Fill in the missing verb forms.

Verb Forms

	Present	Past	Perfect
1.	bring, brings		
2.	come, comes		
3.	feel, feels		
4.	find, finds		
5.	forget, forgets		
6.	get, gets		
7.	hear, hears		
8.	make, makes		
9.	take, takes		

Verb Forms

	Present	Past	Perfect
10.	have, has		
11.	ring, rings		
12.	sing, sings		
13.	swing, swings		
14.	sting, stings		
15.	tear, tears		
16.	swear, swears		
17.	bite, bites		
18.	freeze, freezes		

END OF LESSON 64

A FORM AND USE PERFECT TENSE

Irregular verb — sell

	Present	Past
Simple	sell, sells	sold
Perfect	has sold have sold	had sold

B Fill in the missing verb forms.

Verb Forms

	Present	Past	Perfect		Present	Past	Perfect
1.	pay, pays			15.	get, gets		
2.	say, says			16.	hear, hears		
3.	run, runs			17.	make, makes		
4.	put, puts			18.	take, takes		
5.	sell, sells			19.	has, have		
6.	tell, tells			20.	ring, rings		
7.	sit, sits			21.	sing, sings		
8.	sleep, sleeps			22.	swing, swings		
9.	speak, speaks			23.	sting, stings		
10.	bring, brings			24.	tear, tears		
11.	come, comes			25.	swear, swears		
12.	feel, feels			26.	bite, bites		
13.	find, finds			27.	freeze, freezes		
14.	forget, forgets						

C DETERMINE THE MEANING OF WORDS

Passage
   The heat wave lasted for almost a month. On most days, the temperature was in the 90s and the skies were cloudless. By the end of the heat spell, many younger trees **languished.** Their branches drooped, and their leaves wilted.

1. What part of speech is **languish?** _____

2. What does **languish** probably mean? _____
   _____

3. What information in the passage helped you figure out what **languish** means? _____
   _____

Stop

4. Look up **languish** in the dictionary and write one word that tells what it means in the passage.
   _____

INDEPENDENT WORK

D **Some of the sentences are unclear. Rewrite those sentences so they are clear.**

1. She buys more at a grocery store than a gas station.
   _____

2. She works faster in the morning than her brother.
   _____

3. Our dog eats more dry dog food than table scraps.
   _____

4. Our dog eats more than our cat.
   _____

5. She wanted to do more painting than gymnastics.
   _____

6. Sidney painted more than his little brother.
   _____

7. Jenny planted more in the garden than the window box.
   _____

END OF LESSON 65

A. Fill in the missing verb forms.

Verb Forms

	Present	Past	Perfect
1.	read, reads		
2.	hear, hears		
3.	leave, leaves		
4.	let, lets		
5.	meet, meets		
6.	swim, swims		
7.	stand, stands		
8.	understand, understands		

B. USE ADJECTIVES

Words that come before a noun and make a noun more specific are adjectives. Adjectives answer these questions about nouns:

What kind?
How many?
Which?
Whose?

a. Brave men — What kind of men?
b. Six men — How many men?
c. Those men — Which men?
d. Our men and women — Whose men and women?

Nouns function as adjectives when they give details about another noun.

e. The chicken shed — What kind of shed?
f. The ball park — What kind of park?
g. A snow goose — What kind of goose?
h. A rock truck — What kind of truck?

Lesson 66

C Underline the adjectives.

1. This shark tank contains some little brown creatures.

2. Those four steel beams were made of solid steel.

3. These grass baskets can be filled with rose petals.

4. That huge elephant can eat whole tree branches.

INDEPENDENT WORK

D Fill in the missing verb forms.

Verb Forms

	Present	Past	Perfect		Present	Past	Perfect
1.	pay, pays			15.	get, gets		
2.	say, says			16.	hear, hears		
3.	run, runs			17.	make, makes		
4.	put, puts			18.	take, takes		
5.	sell, sells			19.	has, have		
6.	tell, tells			20.	ring, rings		
7.	sit, sits			21.	sing, sings		
8.	sleep, sleeps			22.	swing, swings		
9.	speak, speaks			23.	sting, stings		
10.	bring, brings			24.	tear, tears		
11.	come, comes			25.	swear, swears		
12.	feel, feels			26.	bite, bites		
13.	find, finds			27.	freeze, freezes		
14.	forget, forgets						

Lesson 66

E. Write a new vocabulary word above each underlined word.

Word list: ubiquitous melee nefarious
languish dissipate extricate

1. The crowd became so angry with the referee's decision that they stormed the field and created a free-for-all fight.

2. The river was so dry that the plants were wilting.

3. The weed seeds scattered in the wind.

4. The person who walked into the shop had a very evil look about him.

5. Internet connections these days are so common that a person is never without one.

END OF LESSON 66

A FORM AND USE PERFECT TENSE

Irregular verb — hear

	Present	Past
Simple	hear, hears	heard
Perfect	has heard	had heard
	have heard	

B Fill in the missing verb forms.

Verb Forms

	Present	Past	Perfect
1.	read, reads		
2.	hear, hears		
3.	leave, leaves		
4.	let, lets		
5.	meet, meets		
6.	swim, swims		
7.	stand, stands		
8.	understand, understands		

C USE ADJECTIVES

Words that come before a noun and make a noun more specific are adjectives. Adjectives answer these questions about nouns:

What kind?
How many?
Which?
Whose?

a. Red roses — What kind of roses?
b. Few roses — How many roses?
c. The roses — Which roses?
d. Mom's roses — Whose roses?

Nouns become adjectives when they answer the questions: **What kind? Whose?**

e. The bicycle tire — What kind of tire?
f. The bicycle's tire — Whose tire?
g. The horse shoes
h. The horse's shoes
i. The shark tank
j. The shark's tank

D Underline the adjectives.

1. His generous father took us to the expensive game.

2. A race horse runs in races.

3. The boys' team won the Smith Trophy.

4. Mike's favorite tennis shoes are worn out.

5. The horse race was scheduled for tomorrow.

END OF LESSON 67

68 Name _____

A USE CONCRETE DETAILS AND DESCRIPTION

Here's the rule about words with apostrophes that answer the question **whose:**

You read the part before the apostrophe. That tells you whether the word refers to **one** or **more than one.**

> The car's brakes are worn.
>
> The cars' brakes are worn.

Remember, find the part before the apostrophe. That part tells you if the word refers to one or more than one.

B Circle *one* or *more than one* to indicate the number that the word with an apostrophe refers to.

> a. The sunset's color was red.
> b. The bricks' color was red.

1. The boys' boats were in the water.

   one   more than one

2. The clown's balloon was huge.

   one   more than one

3. The dogs' howling frightened the scouts.

   one   more than one

4. The groups' grade was very high.

   one   more than one

5. My brothers' dog did amazing tricks.

   one   more than one

6. The rock's weight was more than 80 pounds.

   one   more than one

7. The stars' brilliance was amazing.

     one   more than one

8. The ship's guns were silent.

     one   more than one

C DETERMINE THE MEANING OF WORDS

> *Passage 1*
> Maria is having a meeting next month to discuss possible solutions to the parking problems. This week, she will **disseminate** information about possible solutions to everyone in the neighborhood. She wants to make sure everyone has the information before the meeting.

1. What part of speech is **disseminate**? _____

2. What does **disseminate** probably mean? _____
   _____

3. What words in the passage helped you figure out what **disseminate** means?
   _____

Stop

4. What does **disseminate** mean according to the dictionary?
   _____

Lesson 68   **149**

Passage 2
   Because of the **dearth** of information about the new chemical, he could write only a very short report.

1. What part of speech is **dearth**? _____

2. What does **dearth** probably mean? _____
   _____

3. What words in the passage helped you figure out what **dearth** means? _____
   _____

Stop

4. What does **dearth** mean according to the dictionary? _____
   _____

D FORM AND USE PERFECT TENSE

He lets me out.
She reads books.
We meet at noon.
They stand still.

E Complete each sentence by writing the correct verb.

1. She stands on a rocky slope.

   Simple past: She _____ on a rocky slope.

   Present perfect: She _____ on a rocky slope.

   Past perfect: She _____ on a rocky slope.

2. He swims long distances.

   Simple past: He _____ long distances.

   Present perfect: He _____ long distances.

   Past perfect: He _____ long distances.

3. They hear the news.

   Simple past: They _____ the news.

   Present perfect: They _____ the news.

   Past perfect: They _____ the news.

4. An owl meets a mouse.

   Simple past: An owl _____ a mouse.

   Present perfect: An owl _____ a mouse.

   Past perfect: An owl _____ a mouse.

5. That train leaves at noon.

   Simple past: That train _____ at noon.

   Present perfect: That train _____ at noon.

   Past perfect: That train _____ at noon.

6. He lets me use his bicycle.

   Simple past: He _____ me use his bicycle.

   Present perfect: He _____ me use his bicycle.

   Past perfect: He _____ me use his bicycle.

7. She reads a lot.

   Simple past: She _____ a lot.

   Present perfect: She _____ a lot.

   Past perfect: She _____ a lot.

INDEXPENDENT WORK

F Fill in the missing verb forms.

Verb Forms

	Present	Past	Perfect
1.	pay, pays		
2.	say, says		
3.	run, runs		
4.	put, puts		
5.	sell, sells		
6.	tell, tells		
7.	sit, sits		
8.	sleep, sleeps		
9.	speak, speaks		
10.	bring, brings		
11.	come, comes		
12.	feel, feels		
13.	find, finds		
14.	forget, forgets		

	Present	Past	Perfect
15.	get, gets		
16.	hear, hears		
17.	make, makes		
18.	take, takes		
19.	has, have		
20.	ring, rings		
21.	sing, sings		
22.	swing, swings		
23.	sting, stings		
24.	tear, tears		
25.	swear, swears		
26.	bite, bites		
27.	freeze, freezes		

G. Write a new vocabulary word above each underlined word.

Word list: ubiquitous languish dissipate
extricate melee

1. They are not organized, so all the energy they put in the task is used up.

2. The rabbit was caught in the trap and could not free itself.

3. The two teams met at the middle of the playing field. It started as an argument and ended as a wild fight.

4. The corn grew well until the middle of July, when it began to wilt.

5. The school she came from had three or four rules, but the rules at the new school were everywhere.

END OF LESSON 68

A For each set, circle the letter of the sentence that is written correctly.

Set 1
a. Fred take a good picture.
b. Fred takes a good picture.
c. Fred takes a good picture
d. Fred has took a good picture.

Set 2
a. He runned all the way home yesterday.
b. He is running all the way home yesterday.
c. He ran all the way home yesterday.
d. He run all the way home yesterday.

Set 3
a. He left his work station because he needed a break.
b. He left his work station because he needs a break.
c. He leaves his work station because he needed a break.
d. He leaves his work station because he will need a break.

Set 4
a. She loves to drive a big car but she takes the little one sometimes.
b. She love to drive a big car, but she take the little one sometimes.
c. She loved to drive a big car but she will take the little one sometimes.
d. She loves to drive a big car, but she takes the little one sometimes.

Set 5
a. We doesn't finish the job yesterday but did today.
b. We didn't finish the job yesterday but did today.
c. We didn't finish the job yesterday, but did today.
d. We didn't finish the job yesterday but didn't today.

B PUNCTUATE POSSESSIVES CORRECTLY

> **Its,** the adjective, has no apostrophe. **It's,** the contraction, has an apostrophe.
> **It's** is a contraction for **it is,** a pronoun and a verb. The apostrophe means the letter **I** is left out.
>
> a. The car's brakes are worn.   Whose brakes?
> b. Its brakes are worn.   Whose brakes?
> c. It's time to go.
> d. The dog chewed its tail.
>
> Remember, the only time you write an apostrophe in the word **it's** is when it's a contraction that means **it is.**

Write its or it's in each blank.

1. _____ too hot.

2. The house has _____ own well.

3. _____ the day the building will cast _____ longest shadow.

4. _____ batteries are charged by power from that circulating wheel.

5. That wild dog chased _____ own long tail.

6. _____ raining.

C Circle one or more than one to indicate the number that the word with an apostrophe refers to.

1. The computers' power supply failed.

    one   more than one

2. The boat's engines made a terrible noise.

    one   more than one

3. The animal's tricks amazed the crowd.

    one   more than one

4. The students' paper was well written.

    one   more than one

Lesson 69

5. The girls' notebooks fell off the shelf.

                      one   more than one

6. My cousins' clothes got very muddy.

                      one   more than one

D   **Rewrite each sentence so no words have an apostrophe. Use either its or their to replace the words with an apostrophe.**

its	one
their	more than one

1. The computers' power supply failed.

   _____

2. The boat's engines made a terrible noise.

   _____

3. The animal's tricks amazed the crowd.

   _____

4. The students' paper was well written.

   _____

5. The girls' notebooks fell off the shelf.

   _____

6. My cousins' clothes got very muddy.

   _____

Lesson 69

INDEPENDENT WORK

 Fill in the missing verb forms.

Verb Forms

	Present	Past	Perfect
1.	pay, pays		
2.	say, says		
3.	run, runs		
4.	put, puts		
5.	sell, sells		
6.	tell, tells		
7.	sit, sits		
8.	sleep, sleeps		
9.	speak, speaks		
10.	bring, brings		
11.	come, comes		
12.	feel, feels		
13.	find, finds		
14.	forget, forgets		

	Present	Past	Perfect
15.	get, gets		
16.	hear, hears		
17.	make, makes		
18.	take, takes		
19.	has, have		
20.	ring, rings		
21.	sing, sings		
22.	swing, swings		
23.	sting, stings		
24.	tear, tears		
25.	swear, swears		
26.	bite, bites		
27.	freeze, freezes		

Lesson 69

F Write a new vocabulary word above each underlined word.

Word list: estimate placid nefarious
ubiquitous extricate melee
languish dearth

1. She <u>guessed</u> that the tank could hold 15 gallons.

2. The clothesline broke in the wind and Janice had trouble <u>freeing</u> herself from the tangle of clothes and clotheslines.

3. The <u>shortage</u> of medicine made treatment difficult.

4. The gentlemen disagreed, started yelling at each other, and then engaged in a <u>knock-down fight</u>.

5. He seemed to be quiet and <u>calm</u>, but he had a terrible temper.

6. The organization had a reputation of telling <u>evil</u> lies.

END OF LESSON 69

Name _____

70

A USE SOURCES

Questions

Check the boxes to match each source with the idea or ideas that it supports. Some ideas may have more than one source. Some ideas may have no source.

	Source 1	Source 2	Neither
1. How many tourists were involved in taking the baby bison? _____	☐	☐	☐
2. How old was the baby bison? _____	☐	☐	☐
3. What do the ranger stations do with lost animals in this country? _____	☐	☐	☐
4. How many lost animals a year do tourists bring to ranger stations? _____	☐	☐	☐
5. Why did the tourists not call the ranger station before picking up the baby? _____	☐	☐	☐
6. What happened to the baby bison? _____	☐	☐	☐
7. How much did this mistake cost the tourists? _____	☐	☐	☐

Lesson 70

B UNDERSTAND POSSESSIVES

a. The computers' power supply failed.
b. The boat's engines made a terrible noise.
c. The animal's tricks amazed the crowd.
d. The students' paper was well written.

C Rewrite the sentence so it has the word of and no apostrophe.

1. The chimneys' smoke covered the city.
   _____

2. The rabbit's paws were pink.
   _____

3. The tree's colors changed quickly.
   _____

4. The groups' arguments sounded confusing.
   _____

D USE ADVERBS

- Some words are **adverbs**. Adverbs tell **where** or **when** or **how**.
- Here are sentences that end with adverbs:
    They went **north**. **North** tells **where**. It's an adverb.
    They went **today**. **Today** tells **when**. It's an adverb.
    They went **slowly**. **Slowly** tells **how**. It's an adverb.
- Remember, if a word tells **where, when,** or **how,** it's an adverb.

E Label the part of speech of the last word in the sentence. AV for adverb. N for noun.

1. The workers moved dirt.
2. The workers moved quickly.
3. The dogs barked yesterday.
4. The girls looked east.
5. The scientists watched animals.
6. The cats went home.
7. My mother bought milk.
8. The hunters watched birds.
9. Her eyes looked up.
10. Tracy traveled alone.
11. She kept turning around.

F For each set, circle the letter of the sentence that is written correctly.

Set 1
a. Those dogs runs in the street.
b. Those dogs running in the street.
c. Those dogs run in the street
d. Those dogs run in the street.

Set 2
a. My sister and John talk too much.
b. My sister and John talks too much.
c. My sister and John is talking too much.
d. My sister and John is talks too much.

Set 3
a. A sunny day at the beach.
b. I love a sunny day at the beach.
c. I love a sunny day at the beach with lots of people watching
d. A beautiful, spectacular, sunny day at the beach.

Set 4
a. His lawyer call me when there is a problem.
b. His lawyer calls me when there is a problem.
c. His lawyer calls me, when there is a problem.
d. His lawyer call me, when there is a problem.

Set 5
a. The best players usually gets to start first.
b. The best players usually getting to start first.
c. The best players usually get to start first.
d. The best players usually gots to start first.

INDEPENDENT WORK

G Rewrite the second sentence in each item so the meaning is clear.

1. Mary didn't want to drive to the park. Her suggestion was riding the bus.

2. Dan didn't accept the teacher's explanation. His strategy was arguing for more evidence.

3. The students were deciding what to do. Fran's choice was playing soccer instead of swimming.

H Write a new vocabulary word above each underlined word.

> **Word list:** estimate placid nefarious
> ubiquitous extricate melee
> languish dearth

1. She found a <u>shortage</u> of information about the new proposal.

2. The person walking to the door looked <u>wicked</u>. So we hid and pretended we weren't home.

Lesson 70

3. She made a good <u>guess</u> about the number of people coming to the event. We had only two extra chairs.

4. The sea was so <u>calm</u>. The surface was like glass.

5. Rain is <u>common</u> in the tropics.

I   **Fill in each blank with it's or its. Remember, the only time you write an apostrophe in the word it's is when it's a contraction that means it is.**

1. _____ a long way to Billtown.

2. When _____ raining, _____ hair gets wet.

3. I know _____ the best way to stop _____ leak.

4. _____ wheels are fixed.

END OF LESSON 70

A DETERMINE THE MEANING OF WORDS

> 1. My mother **proscribed** my plan for spending her money, so I had to forget about buying that furniture.

1. What part of speech is **proscribed?** _____

2. What does **proscribed** probably mean? _____
_____

3. What other words in the passage helped you figure out what **proscribed** means? _____
_____

Stop

4. What does **proscribed** mean according to the dictionary?
_____

> 2. The **exclusive** report was on channel WBTQ, so you'll have to go to that channel to get the news.

1. What part of speech is **exclusive?** _____

2. What does **exclusive** probably mean? _____
_____

3. What other words in the passage helped you figure out what **exclusive** means? _____
_____

Stop

4. What does **exclusive** mean according to the dictionary?
_____

INDEPENDENT WORK

B Fill in the missing verb forms.

Verb Forms

	Present	Past	Perfect
1.	pay, pays		
2.	say, says		
3.	run, runs		
4.	put, puts		
5.	sell, sells		
6.	tell, tells		
7.	sit, sits		
8.	sleep, sleeps		
9.	speak, speaks		
10.	bring, brings		
11.	come, comes		
12.	feel, feels		
13.	find, finds		
14.	forget, forgets		

	Present	Past	Perfect
15.	get, gets		
16.	hear, hears		
17.	make, makes		
18.	take, takes		
19.	has, have		
20.	ring, rings		
21.	sing, sings		
22.	swing, swings		
23.	sting, stings		
24.	tear, tears		
25.	swear, swears		
26.	bite, bites		
27.	freeze, freezes		

C Fill in each blank with <u>it's</u> or <u>its</u>. Remember, the only time you write an apostrophe in the word it's is when it's a contraction that means <u>it is</u>.

1. _____ easy.

2. _____ never too late.

3. The dog ate _____ food.

4. _____ better to let it take _____ time.

END OF LESSON 71

Lesson 71 **165**

A USE ADVERBS AND ADJECTIVES

> Some of these sentences end with an **adverb.** Some end with an **adjective.**
>
> You've learned that **adjectives** make nouns more specific by answering the question **what kind, how many, which,** or **whose.**
>
> Here's how to test whether the last word is an adjective: Say the noun in the subject with the last word of the sentence in front of it. If it makes sense, the last word is an adjective.
>
> **The vehicle was slow.**
> **slow vehicle**
>
> **Slow vehicle** makes sense. **Slow** tells what kind of vehicle. So **slow** is an **adjective.**

B Label the part of speech of the last word in each sentence, <u>A</u> for adjective, <u>AV</u> for adverb.

1. The picture looked interesting.

2. The birds looked around.

3. The birds looked beautiful.

4. The work was difficult.

5. The shadows became longer.

6. The sun went down.

7. Five children were there.

8. Those sentences seem complicated.

9. Many birds flew together.

10. The workers felt tired.

INDEPENDENT WORK

C Write a new vocabulary word above each underlined word.

> *Word list:* estimate placid nefarious
> ubiquitous extricate melee
> languish dearth proscribe
> exclusive

1. Ross had no evil intention, but his report resulted in a huge loss of votes for our position.

2. The shortage of chairs meant that most everyone stood.

3. The bureau voted to reject the use of motorized vehicles on the path.

4. We have the only admission to the program.

5. The monkeys were everywhere in the rain forest.

D Fill in each blank with it's or its. Remember, the only time you write an apostrophe in the word it's is when it's a contraction that means it is.

1. _____ going to rain.

2. _____ color is a beautiful blue.

3. _____ not hard.

4. _____ a good deal, and _____ not too late.

END OF LESSON 72

74

A DETERMINE THE MEANING OF WORDS

> **Passage 1**
> Marco had a box of chocolates to share. Maria said, "I'm **partial to** dark chocolate." Marco nodded as Maria helped herself to dark chocolate.

1. What part of speech is **partial to**? _____

2. What does it probably mean to be **partial to** something? _____

3. What other words in the passage helped you figure out what it means to be **partial to** something? _____

Stop

4. What does **partial to** mean according to the dictionary? _____

5. What's another way of saying, **Rollo likes basketball better than other sports?** _____

> **Passage 2**
> Most members agreed that the reports contained too much **incidental** material. So the committee agreed to shorten the reports and focus on only important material.

1. What part of speech is **incidental**? _____

2. What does **incidental** probably mean? _____

3. What other words in the passage helped you figure out what **incidental** means? _____

Lesson 74

Stop

4. What does **incidental** mean according to the dictionary?

_____

5. What's another way saying, **The judge's criticisms were unimportant?**

_____

B USE ADVERBS AND ADJECTIVES

> You have learned to test nouns, adjectives, and adverbs that are at the end of sentences.
>
> Remember, a **noun** makes sense with the word **one** or **some** in front of it.
>
> You test **adjectives** by seeing if the word tells about the **noun** in the subject.
>
> **Adjectives** tell **what kind, how many, which,** or **whose** about a noun.
>
> **Adverbs** tell **how, when,** or **where.**
>
> My sister will visit us tomorrow.
Tomorrow sister
>
> **Tomorrow** doesn't tell **what kind** of sister. **Tomorrow** tells **when.**

Label the part of speech of the last word in each sentence: N for noun, A for adjective, and AV for adverb.

1. My sister will visit Henry.

2. My sister visits often.

3. My sister is friendly.

4. My sister gets nervous.

5. My sister gets rashes.

6. My sister stays inside.

7. My sister washes clothes.

8. My sister washes often.

Lesson 74

INDEPENDENT WORK

C Draw a line over the joining word. Circle the subjects. Underline the key verbs. On the line, write the number of clauses in the sentence. Then circle the tense.

1. Those animals are running from flies before the rain comes. ____

   past   present

2. The campers were walking home until someone gave them a ride. ____

   past   present

3. They were arguing until midnight. ____

   past   present

4. He is mowing the lawn while the sun is shining. ____

   past   present

D Rewrite each sentence. Use either its, his, her, or their to replace each word with an apostrophe.

1. The birds' song was loud.
   _____

2. The bird's song was loud.
   _____

3. John's habits are disgusting.
   _____

4. My cousins' habits are disgusting.
   _____

5. Those boys' tents were yellow.
   _____

6. The girls' dresses were yellow.
   _____

7. The girl's brother was mean.
   _____

END OF LESSON 74

A Label the part of speech for all the words in each sentence. <u>N</u> for noun, <u>V</u> for verb, <u>A</u> for adjective, and <u>AV</u> for adverb.

1. My cat eats frequently.

2. My cat is gray.

3. My cat sleeps there.

4. My cat eats fish.

5. My cat went out.

6. My cat jumps around.

7. My cat chases mice.

8. My cat is sleepy.

B **DETERMINE THE MEANING OF WORDS**

Passage 1
   His story was so **vivid** that the audience felt they were in the story, participating in the events as they unfolded.

1. What part of speech is **vivid**? _____

2. What does **vivid** probably mean? _____
   _____

3. What other words in the passage helped you figure out what **vivid** means?
   _____

Lesson 75 171

Stop

4. What synonym for **vivid** works best in this context?
_____

5. What's another way of saying this sentence: **The colors in the painting were so lifelike.**
_____

> **Passage 2**
> Some people told him that he spoke with too much **candor.** For that reason, he decided against telling exactly what he thought.

1. What part of speech is **candor?** _____

2. What does **candor** probably mean? _____
_____

3. What other words in the passage helped you figure out what **candor** means?
_____

Stop

4. What synonym for **candor** works best in this context?
_____

5. What's another way of saying this sentence: **The boy spoke with honesty about his feelings.**
_____

6. What's another way of saying this sentence: **I prefer chocolate.**
_____

Lesson 75

INDEPENDENT WORK

C Write a new vocabulary word above each underlined word.

> **Word list:** terse   demure   dearth
> proscribed   exclusive   partial to
> incidental

1. Mani prefers fancy events.

2. The ladies in the room were very quiet and polite.

3. The boy answered the question with a very brief, "I don't remember."

4. The report was full of unimportant information.

5. Bright Cinema has the only rights to show the movie.

6. Most birds prefer sunflower seeds.

END OF LESSON 75

Name _____

A WRITE INFORMATIVE TEXT

Questions

1. Check the boxes to match each source with the idea or ideas that it supports. Some ideas may have more than one source selected.

	Source 1	Source 2
a. Thousands of pieces of junk are in space.	☐	☐
b. Space junk is the litter of previous space missions.	☐	☐
c. Shuttles have steered around junk once or twice a year.	☐	☐

Write your answers to questions 2 and 3 on your lined paper.

2. Which source has the most useful information about where space junk comes from? Support your answer by telling two details from that source about the origin of space junk.

Outline Diagram

> Source __ tells [use words from the question]. Source __ states that [give one reason]. Source __ also states that [   ].

3. Explain why space junk is a problem. Give **two** reasons, one from Source #1 and one from Source #2. For each reason, include the source title or number.

Outline Diagram

> [Use words from the item.] Source 1 states that [   ].
> Source 2 states that [   ].

B
Label the part of speech for each word. Write A for adjective, N for noun, V for verb, and AV for adverb.

1. Five girls came here.

2. Green butterflies are rare.

3. Some boys are energetic.

4. Those young women teach engineers.

5. The delivery person is late.

6. Her dad speaks often.

7. Your oldest sister left yesterday.

8. Their document presented information.

C USE COMMAS CORRECTLY

> Some words are not part of the subject or the predicate of a sentence. You set off those words with a comma.

a. Do you want more chicken?
b. Steve, do you want more chicken?
c. Are you happy?
d. Are you happy Alex?

D
Put commas in all the sentences that need them.

1. Andy stand next to your mother.

2. That picture was drawn by Hank.

3. Give your sister a hand Michael.

4. Robin and Martha where were you yesterday?

5. Turn off the TV Eric.

6. Did Eric or somebody else turn off the TV?

7. Susie did you finish your homework?

INDEPENDENT WORK

E Label the part of speech of each word in the sentence.

1. The girl kissed her mother.

2. The girl followed John.

3. The girl looked up.

4. The picture was vivid.

F Write a new vocabulary word for each underlined word.

> **Word list:**   terse   demure   dearth
> proscribed   exclusive   partial to
> incidental   vivid   candor

1. It was clear that the boy told the story with honesty.

2. The storyteller could make a story come alive with lifelike details.

3. The teacher rejected passes to the restroom during class.

4. The shortage of wildlife in the park was due to the lack of rain.

5. She is fond of sunbathing during her vacation.

END OF LESSON 76

A   USE COMMAS TO SET OFF WORDS

You've learned interjections are words that show a burst of emotion. Here are some interjections:

oh my	ouch	well	gosh
wow	okay	no	yes
hey	oops	oh	darn

Interjections can be added to a sentence. They are not a part of the subject or the predicate of a sentence, so you separate them from the rest of the sentence with commas.

I lost my wallet, darn.
Wow, that was a big blast!
Ouch, that hurts!
Yes, that's right.
Hey, what are you doing?

B   Place commas in all these sentences.

1. No I won't go there.

2. Oh you surprised me.

3. I'm not sure what I'll do darn.

4. Yes I think you're correct.

5. He said, "Okay I'll do it."

6. Wow that's one strong smell.

C Label the part of speech of all the words in each sentence.

1. The horse was awkward.
2. Those white birds are doves.
3. Billy swims well.
4. That red car is Billy's.
5. Our six candles burned quickly.
6. That stove burns damp logs.
7. Chimneys gather soot.
8. Our assignment was difficult.
9. Those barking dogs are Tony's.
10. The work is his.

INDEPENDENT WORK

D Place commas in the sentences to separate words that are not part of the subject or predicate.

1. Tia are you coming?
2. Help Rosa with the dishes will you?
3. Let's take Hank with us.
4. Suki and Togo when are you coming?
5. Turn off the stove Emma.
6. Did Emma or Maria turn off the stove?
7. Quit making faces Maddie!

END OF LESSON 77

A Put commas where they should be for each item.

> **Example**
> I told you Ann the party starts at 4.
> I told you, Ann, the party starts at 4.

1. Did you ask Don or Sally?

2. Why are you smiling, Ginger?

3. I told you, Vern, we didn't go there last night.

4. Well, what do you think?

5. Wow, that's a good sentence!

6. I told you three times, Herb, that I'll help you.

7. If he calls me soon, boy, I'll be so happy!

B Label the part of speech for all the words in each sentence.

1. She is pretty.

2. He runs quickly.

3. Those boxes hold cups.

4. He is strong.

5. Seven curious ducks looked around.

6. The neighbors argued loudly.

INDEPENDENT WORK

C **Place commas in the sentences to separate words that are not part of the subject or predicate.**

1. Yes I want to go with you.

2. Yikes what is that?

3. Oh no we can't make it in time.

4. Tom has the best idea.

5. No that's not right.

6. "Well I will help you if I have time," Anna said.

7. Ouch that needle hurts!

D **Write a new vocabulary word above each underlined word.**

Word list:	demure	aspiration	clad
	estate	exclusive	is partial to
	incidental	vivid	candor
	obstreperous		

1. Toddlers at dinner can be so <u>unruly</u>.

2. I appreciate your <u>honesty</u> in telling me the reasons why you won't be voting for me.

3. His <u>goal</u> was to become a doctor.

4. How you feel about the problem is <u>unimportant</u>. What matters is what the majority thinks.

5. She takes a long time to tell a story, but her stories are always very <u>lifelike</u>.

6. Grandma <u>favors</u> her grandchildren.

END OF LESSON 78

Name _____

A Fill in all the is-verb forms.

Is-Verbs

Subject	Present	Past	Present Perfect	Past Perfect
he, she, it				
we, you, they				
I				

B USE COMMAS TO SET OFF WORDS

It's a beautiful day isn't it?
It's a beautiful day, isn't it?

C Punctuate the sentences.

1. That took a long time didn't it?

2. Wow his sister is amazing!

3. Tell me Hank how did you learn long division?

4. Listen we have to work together.

5. We'll have a good time won't we?

6. I have the best paper don't I?

7. Greg stop asking so many questions.

INDEPENDENT WORK

D Label the part of speech of each word in the sentence.

1. She ate hotdogs.

2. I am obstreperous.

3. Her father walked quickly.

4. The lake was placid.

E Place commas in the sentences to separate words that are not part of the subject or the predicate.

1. He finished first didn't he?

2. "That is a big fish Julio!" Meg exclaimed.

3. When you are ready Helen we can begin.

4. Well I'll just help myself.

5. No I don't want any more soap.

6. That's the best way to get home isn't it?

7. Hanna has her own car.

END OF LESSON 79

Name _____

A   Punctuate the sentence.

1. I explained Mr. Baker that we were not in the park.

2. You do a lot better Glenda when you work harder.

3. Who asked you Helen?

4. Omar why are you smiling so much?

5. Oh my the dog got loose.

6. I'm telling you Ted you have a great plan.

7. I believe in space monsters don't you?

8. Well I'm not sure what to do.

B   Fill in all the is-verb forms.

Is-Verbs

Subject	Present	Past	Present Perfect	Past Perfect
he, she, it				
we, you, they				
I				

Lesson 80

INDEPENDENT WORK

C Label the part of speech of the last word in the sentence: **A** for adjective, **N** for noun, **AV** for adverb.

1. She was beautiful.
2. The fish jumped often.
3. Our building is wooden.
4. Jim purchased goods.
5. All my cousins are carpenters.
6. Andy collected wood.
7. Those boats were light.
8. Our neighbors shopped late.
9. I turned off the light.

D Place commas in the sentences to separate words that are not part of the subject or the predicate.

1. I am telling you Nanna that I can't do it on Tuesday.
2. What do you mean Lucia?
3. I want to go to the party with Pendleton.
4. Sherlock how are you going to find out who did it?
5. I love chocolate don't you?
6. I'm sure Nick that your idea is good.
7. Well let's try it a different way.

END OF LESSON 80

A DRAW EVIDENCE FROM INFORMATIONAL TEXTS

Questions

1. For items a through c, check the boxes to match each source with the idea or ideas that it supports.

	Source 1	Source 2	Source 3
a. Rounding prices will cause a decrease in prices.	☐	☐	☐
b. The low value of a penny is a good thing.	☐	☐	☐
c. Using cheaper metals to make the penny is a better way to cut the cost of a penny.	☐	☐	☐

Write your answers to questions 2 and 3 on your paper.

2. Which sources present evidence for stopping the production and distribution of pennies? Use **one** detail from each source to support your choices. For each detail, include the source title or number.

3. Which sources present evidence against ending production of the penny? Use **at least two** details to support your choices. For each detail, include the source title or number.

Lesson 81

B PREPOSITIONAL PHRASES

Prepositions: of   in   on

1. The tongue of the dog.

2. The cars in the garage.

3. The boys on the team.

4. The girl in the woods.

C Draw a line over the prepositional phrases and write the correct verb, was or were.

> The group of words that start with a preposition and end with a noun is called a prepositional phrase.

1. The girl in the pictures _____ attractive.

2. The numbers on the page _____ large.

3. The possessions of the man _____ lost.

4. The tax on her purchases _____ two dollars.

5. The group of soldiers _____ resting.

6. The flights of our plane _____ exciting.

D IDENTIFY FORMS OF THE IS-VERB

You've learned forms of **is-verbs**.

Here are all the **is-verb** forms:

is   are   am   was   were   have been   has been   had been

You can see sentences with **is-verbs**:

They **were** tired.
She **is** hungry.
I **had been** in town.
Those girls **are** hard workers.
We **have been** to the Jones's several times.
I **am** happy.

The sentences above have verbs that are forms of **is**. **Is-verbs** followed by a word that ends I-N-G are not forms of is anymore.

Form of is-verb	Not an is-verb form
a. She is in the shower.	She is singing in the shower.
b. They have been to the fair.	They have been showing at the fair.
c. We are at the pool.	We are swimming at the pool.
d. The boys had been at the creek.	The boys had been playing at the creek.

Remember, if the last verb word ends **I-N-G,** the verb is not an **is-verb**.

E Underline the verbs in each sentence. Circle the is-verbs.

1. The girls ran fast.

2. The girls were running fast.

3. They have been good friends.

4. The two boys have been playing catch.

5. The two boys were cousins.

6. The cans are rolling down the hill.

7. Those dogs had been seeing-eye dogs.

8. Those dogs are sitting near my house.

9. The cans are red and white.

10. I am running for class president.

11. Susan was asking about the election.

12. I am a good student.

INDEPENDENT WORK

F Fill in the blank boxes with the correct form of the is-verb.

Is-Verbs

Subject	Present	Past	Present Perfect	Past Perfect
he, she, it				
we, you, they				
I				

END OF LESSON 81

A Underline the whole verb in each sentence. Circle all the is-verbs.

1. My sister was sleeping.

2. The girls have been ready.

3. Five dogs stand on our porch.

4. Those dogs were nervous.

5. I am riding my bike.

6. I am in a hurry.

7. The crickets were near the pond.

8. The crickets were making noise.

9. He is asking many questions.

B For each sentence, draw a line over the prepositional phrase and write the correct verb, was or were.

1. The color of our maple trees _____ brilliant.

2. Parts of our car _____ expensive.

3. The gloves on the desk _____ dirty.

4. The effort of the workers _____ impressive.

5. The boys in the car _____ my friends.

Lesson 82

INDEPENDENT WORK

C Fill in the blank boxes with the correct form of the is-verb.

Is-Verbs

Subject	Present	Past	Present Perfect	Past Perfect
he, she, it				
we, you, they				
I				

END OF LESSON 82

Name _____

A Write information to connect the two events in each item.

Some words you can use:

After

During

While

When

1. The basketball tournament went on for hours.

   _____ , we went home for dinner.

2. They had a great day at the beach.

   _____ , they came home very tired.

3. I am going to take the highway to Johnsonville at 2 pm.

   _____ , the city traffic is bad.

4. Our choir was practicing four songs.

   _____ , we made a recording.

END OF LESSON 86

A For each item, the missing verb is either was or were. Rewrite each sentence so it doesn't have the word of. One of the words in each sentence will need an apostrophe.

1. The tables of the lounge _____ too big.
   _____

2. The procedure of the scientists _____ well tested.
   _____

3. The pets of the child _____ well behaved.
   _____

4. The cars of the driver _____ fast.
   _____

5. The sound of the trumpets _____ inspiring.
   _____

INDEPENDENT WORK

B For each item, the missing verb is either was or were. Rewrite each sentence so it doesn't have the word of. One of the words in each sentence will need an apostrophe.

1. The noise of the children _____ deafening.
   _____

2. The walls of Z-Mart _____ made of steel.
   _____

3. The photo of my brother _____ great.
   _____

4. The hobbies of my brothers _____ fun.
   _____

END OF LESSON 87

Name _____

A Draw a line over the prepositional phrases. Some sentences don't have any prepositional phrases.

1. The dogs were locked in the kennel.

2. The dogs were locked in.

3. She saw me and walked on the other side.

4. She saw me and walked on.

5. The janitor turned the lights on in the big building.

6. I want to stay in.

7. I want to stay in the house.

8. I want to stay in now.

END OF LESSON 88

89 Name _____

A Write an ending for each sentence.

1. He ran as fast as _____ .

2. She was as pretty _____ .

3. He moved as quietly _____ .

4. They were as busy _____ .

B Draw a line over all the prepositional phrases in the sentences.

1. The wolves in the forest howl very loudly in the evening.

2. The children in the class were supposed to turn their papers in.

3. The best donuts are served in the bakery on the corner.

4. The children on the playground can't play in the gym.

5. The janitor on duty wanted to turn the lights on.

6. The tallest building in the world is found in Dubai.

7. The players on the team were the fastest runners in the school.

END OF LESSON 89

90

Name _____

A Write an ending for these sentences. Start the ending with the word <u>as</u>.

1. He was as happy _____.

2. Her mother was as busy _____.

3. Her brother was as silly _____.

4. This job is as easy _____.

5. She felt as free _____.

6. The weather was as hot _____.

END OF LESSON 90

A Write good endings for these sentences.

> The part after **or** parallels the part after **either**.
>
> She will either <u>do her homework</u> or _____
>
> **OK:** She will either <u>do her homework</u> or <u>her chores</u>.
>
> **Better:** She will either <u>do her homework</u> or <u>do her chores</u>.
>
> **Another way:** She will do either <u>her homework</u> or <u>her chores</u>.

1. Jim will either fix his bike or _____ .
2. The bus will either be on time _____ .
3. The weather will either improve tomorrow _____ .
4. She will either remodel her house _____ .

B USE ADJECTIVES AND ADVERBS CORRECTLY

You're going to learn more about adjectives and adverbs.

If a word describes a **noun**, it's an **adjective**.

Here's a sentence with the adjectives underlined.

The man's <u>enormous</u> hat was <u>attractive</u>.

The adjectives all describe the noun **hat**.

Adjectives can come before a noun, or they can be in the predicate following an **is**-verb.

If a word describes a **verb**, an **adjective**, or another **adverb**, it's an **adverb**.

Here are sentences with the adverbs underlined.

a. The <u>very</u> enormous hat was <u>quite</u> attractive.
b. He <u>always</u> wears a hat.
c. She walked <u>quickly</u>.
d. She walked <u>very</u> quickly.

The adverbs in sentence a describe adjectives.

The adverb in sentence b describes a verb.

The adverb in sentence c also describes a verb.

The underlined adverb in sentence d describes another adverb.

C Circle the word that each adverb describes and label the part of speech of the word you circled. Circled words can only be verbs (V), adjectives (A), or other adverbs (AV).

1. We just finished our homework.

2. She watched closely as the very big truck backed slowly into our extremely long driveway.

3. That is absolutely delicious.

4. He easily won the game.

5. Don't stop here.

6. He backed away.

7. She walked very slowly to the edge of the cliff.

INDEPENDENT WORK

D Indicate the part of speech for each word.

1. Our old car runs well.

2. The latest newspaper had twenty pages.

3. The new outfit is handsome.

4. They followed us closely.

END OF LESSON 91

92 Name _____

A Circle the word that each adverb describes and label the part of speech of the word you circled. Circled words can only be verbs (V), adjectives (A), or other adverbs (AV).

1. He was happily eating his food.

2. She never takes a short cut.

3. She was unusually strong.

4. He never became angry.

5. We were very happy in our new home.

6. He only eats cereal for breakfast.

7. He quite easily finished first.

B Draw a line over all the prepositional phrases in each sentence.

Prepositions							
in	on	of	under	between	down	without	over
near	after	at	above	around	before	around	before
by	from	to	behind	beside	with		

1. The man from the office found the note hidden behind the bricks.

2. The toys under the stairs are from Grandma.

3. The letter from her brother arrived with a package yesterday.

4. The players from Hill High School were the best around.

5. Five ducks with 47 babies were happily swimming down the river.

6. The nicest people come from Tintown.

7. She really wanted to sit beside Merv.

8. The boy with the curly hair is ready to run around the track.

END OF LESSON 92

Name

A
Draw a line above the prepositional phrases in these sentences and write above the line A for adjective or AV for adverb to indicate the function of the prepositional phrase.

1. He walked in quickly.

2. He walked on the sidewalk.

3. The lady on the phone said that we should pay our bill today.

4. The boat on the river was tilting on its side.

5. The lights in the living room were turned on.

6. My dad came into the kitchen.

7. His dog with white whiskers is very well trained.

B
Write good endings for these sentences.

1. Tom was either totally happy or _____ .

2. His dog was as large as _____ .

3. The garbage collector will either pick up our garbage on Monday _____ .

4. His hands were as big _____ .

C Circle the subject and underline the adverbs in each sentence. Write KV over the key verb.

> Adverbs that usually describe verbs:
> always   usually   never   often

1. My friends always ride the bus.

2. Burt's dog never bites.

3. My friends preferably ride the bus.

4. We never invite the neighbors for tea.

5. They often come to visit.

INDEPENDENT WORK

D Adverbs are underlined. Circle the word that each adverb describes and label it verb (V), adjective (A), or adverb (AV).

1. The Smith brothers are <u>easily</u> spotted in their big cowboy hats.

2. The dessert was <u>indescribably</u> delicious.

3. It was a <u>very</u> smooth ride.

4. I <u>never</u> remember where the turn is.

5. She made her correction <u>very</u> quickly.

END OF LESSON 93

A **Write good endings for these sentences.**

1. When they started the trip, they were neither hungry _____ .

2. The train car was neither smoky _____ .

3. He couldn't go fishing because he had neither fishhooks _____ .

B **Circle the subject and underline the adverbs in each sentence. Write KV over the key verb.**

1. We picked corn in the very hot sun.

2. Our car always causes trouble.

3. Those songs are incredibly melodious.

4. I will never forget you.

5. We always take the bus.

END OF LESSON 94

95 Name _____

A Complete these sentences.

1. Neither her mother _____ thought her joke was funny.

2. Neither snow _____ will stop the mail service.

3. They felt neither cold _____ in the plane.

4. The dog's tail wagged as fast _____ .

5. They will name the new baby either Glen _____ .

6. The rock was as large _____ .

INDEPENDENT WORK

B Circle the word that the underlined adverb describes. Label that word verb (V), adjective (A), or other adverb (AV).

1. I <u>never</u> wished for this.

2. The James girls make the <u>most</u> delicious hamburgers.

3. She <u>only</u> hoped that you would come.

4. He walked <u>very</u> slowly into the barn.

5. The play was <u>very</u> interesting.

6. She has a <u>very</u> big smile.

END OF LESSON 95

Name _____

96

A. LIST DIGITAL SOURCES

This is the format for listing a source:

Author last name, Author first initial. (Year, Month Day). Title. Website address

Matthews, J. (2019, October 19). Plastic Bottles. www.plasticheadaches.com

B. List these sources.

1. Author: Takai Yonono
   Title: The Elderly
   Website: http://www.geriatrics.com
   Number of articles at the website: 17
   Name of the organization that owns the website: Elderly Residence
   Date written: November 4, 2014

   _____

   _____

2. Title: Music for the Heart
   Date written: March 10, 2016
   Name of organization that owns the website: Music Masters
   Website address: http://www.musicmasters.org
   Author's name: Tina Rodriguez

   _____

   _____

3. Title: Fly Fishing in the Outback
   Name of organization that owns the website: Association of Fishermen
   Address of the organization: Boston, Massachusetts
   Website address: http://www.fishermen.org
   Author's name: Smith, Miata
   Date written: 2020

   _____

   _____

END OF LESSON 96

A LIST DIGITAL SOURCES

This is the format for listing a source:

Author last name, Author first initial. (Year, Month Day). Title. Website address

Smith, A. (2011, October 11). Women as Leaders. www.topicsofinterest.com

Richards, T. (n.d.). Better Business. www.bestbusiness.com

List these sources.

1. Author: Diego Verde
   Title: How to Make the Best Tacos
   Website: http://www.mexicancooking.com
   Number of articles on the website: 22
   Name of the organization that owns the website: Mexican Cooking

   _____

2. Title: Animals that are Alive in Zoos but Extinct in the Wild
   Date written: 2017
   Name of organization that owns the website: Zoos for Animal Preservation
   Website address: http://www.zooscience.org
   Author's name: Thomas Zooman

   _____

3. Website address: http://www.oldwest.com
   Name of organization that owns the website: Association of Cowboys
   Address of the organization: Dallas, Texas
   Title: Modern Cowboys
   Author's name: Ronald Longhorn

   _____

4. Title: How to Wash Your Car
   Website address: http://www.tomstricks.org
   Author's name: Nguyen, Haru
   Date written: January 21, 2005

   _____
   _____

B WRITE ENDINGS FOR THESE SENTENCES.

1. Doug didn't know whether he should keep working or
   _____

2. They didn't know whether to take the train to Lakeland
   _____

3. The students couldn't decide whether to work in small groups
   _____

4. Nina wasn't sure whether her plan would fail
   _____

END OF LESSON 97

98

A Complete each sentence.

1. The lake was as blue _____

2. I will either write to my brother _____

3. She didn't know whether she should cry _____

4. They will either shop at the mall _____

5. I couldn't decide whether to take a break _____

6. The man's muscles were as hard _____

7. Her brother didn't know whether to wait one hour _____
   _____ before swimming.

8. Neither mountains _____
   _____ are flat.

END OF LESSON 98

Name _____

99

A
Draw a line above the prepositional phrases in these sentences and write above the line A for adjective or AV for adverb to indicate the function of the prepositional phrase.

> **More prepositions:**
> between   for   in   to   from   around

1. The box between the trees is used for trash.
2. The bees in the hive were ready for the flowers.
3. The boys from Newtown walked around the field to find a lost ball.
4. We walked to the new swimming pool.
5. The best things in life are free.

INDEPENDENT WORK

B
Complete these sentences.

1. Neither the cows _____ were well fed.
2. The lake was as blue _____.
3. I will either write to my brother _____.
4. She didn't know whether she should cry _____.
5. They will either shop at the mall _____.
6. I couldn't decide whether to take a break _____.
7. The man's muscles were as hard _____.
8. Her brother didn't know whether to wait one hour _____ before swimming.
9. Neither mountains _____ are flat.

END OF LESSON 99

101 Name _____

A **Draw lines to connect the figures of speech in the right column to the sentences in the left column.**

1. She didn't cry when she heard the bad news. She was ____ .

2. He was cleaning the house, vacuuming, and dusting at the same time. He was ____ .

3. He never told a lie, no matter what. He was ____ .

4. She would tell one story when an entirely different story was true. She was ____ .

5. We saw so many Bumpo cars on the freeway. Bumpos were ____ .

6. Her purse was empty. So it was ____ .

7. She was so dramatic about everything and everyone knew who she was. She was ____ .

- slept like a log.
- as free as a bird.
- larger than life.
- as light as a feather.
- as tough as nails.
- as plain as day.
- as quick as a wink.
- as slippery as an eel.
- as busy as a bee.
- as straight as an arrow.
- as smooth as silk.
- as common as dirt.

B In the box, write the number of the first paragraph in the story that answers each question. Then write the answer to the question.

1. Who are the two main characters of the story? ☐
   _____

2. What's the name of the third character in the story? ☐
   _____

3. What did Ted find most difficult? ☐
   _____

4. How did he prepare himself? ☐
   _____

5. What happened when Ted was just about ready to ask Amy to go to the prom with him? ☐
   _____

6. What did Ted think about Amy's reaction to Jamal? ☐
   _____
   _____

7. Did Ted succeed in his most difficult task? ☐
   _____

8. Now that Ted is 32 years old, what does he still regret? ☐
   _____

END OF LESSON 101

Lesson 101

103 Name _____

A Draw lines to connect the figures of speech in the right column to the sentences in the left column.

1. He was so happy to have a vacation. He felt ___ .

2. She finished cleaning the car in just a few minutes. She was ___ .

3. After he washed the garage out, the garage was ___ .

4. He was so tired after the long hike. As soon as he laid down he ___ .

5. After he shaves, my dad's face is was ___ .

6. She had difficulty finding her keys when they were easy to see. They were ___ .

7. He was a very lively personality. Everyone watched him. He was ___ .

- slept like a log.
- as free as a bird.
- larger than life.
- as light as a feather.
- as tough as nails.
- as plain as day.
- as quick as a wink.
- as slippery as an eel.
- as busy as a bee.
- as clean as a whistle.
- as smooth as silk.
- as common as dirt.

END OF LESSON 103

Name _____

A UNDERSTAND SIMILES AND METAPHORS

a. She has a heart of gold.

b. You are my sunshine.

c. That boy is a pig.

d. Mortimer is a big chicken. He won't try the skate park.

B Draw lines to connect the figures of speech in the left column to the correct descriptions in the right column that fit each figure of speech.

1. being chicken • • He talked about how smart he was but he didn't do well in school.

2. a couch potato • • afraid to take risks

3. a pig • • inactive, watch tv a lot

4. heart of gold • • sloppy, messy

5. a phony baloney • • generous, thoughtful

C In the box, write the number of the first paragraph in the story that answers each question. Then write the answer to the question.

1. Who are the two main characters of the story? ☐

_____

2. What two events made John happy? ☐

_____

3. Where was Murry going? ☐

_____

Lesson 104   211

4. What kind of job did Murry have for years? ☐
   _____

5. How long has it been since Murry has done this kind of work? ☐
   _____

6. What evidence shows that the man sitting beside Murry on the subway was not comfortable with Murry's coughing? ☐
   _____

7. Why did Murry cough? ☐
   _____

8. What was John London planning to do when he got home? ☐
   _____

9. What was Murry planning to do when he arrived at his destination? ☐
   _____

END OF LESSON 104

A Draw lines to connect the figures of speech with the correct meaning.

1. slept like a log • • He was over six feet tall and weighed less than 120 pounds. He was ___ .

2. blue diamonds • • The cake was so light, it was ___ .

3. a toothpick • • Her eyes were a beautiful light blue. They were ___ .

4. as a feather • • I felt very glad to get out of that old house. I felt free as ___ .

5. a bird • • He worked from sunrise to sunset. When he went to bed that evening he ___ .

B CITE EVIDENCE IN LITERARY TEXTS

You've learned how to write quote marks around the exact words people said in a story.

You've also put quote marks around words that you copied from an article.

You're going learn how to use quote marks to identify evidence to support a statement you make about a story.

The story text in paragraph 5:

Nobody knew what happened to Roger.

Sentence a quotes evidence from the story:

a. It states in paragraph 5, "Nobody knew what happened to Roger."

Sentence b shows the same sentence with only the word **that** added. Because sentence b has the word **that,** there is no comma and no capital at the beginning of the quote:

b. It states in paragraph 5 that "nobody knew what happened to Roger."

Sentence c shows the sentence with the word **that** and more words added.

c. It states in paragraph 5 that nobody from the Smith family "knew what happened to Roger."

Sentence c makes clear who "nobody" refers to from previous information in the story.

When you identify evidence for a point you want to make about a story, you focus on specific information given in the story. You put quote marks around the exact words from the story and tell the location. The words in sentences b and c that are exactly the same as the story text have quote marks around them.

Lesson 105   213

Place quote marks and capital letters in these statements that identify evidence from a story.

Story text in paragraph 6: They were eager to hear the news.

Statements identifying evidence:

1. It states in paragraph 6 they were eager to hear the news.

2. It states in paragraph 6 that they were eager to hear the news.

3. It states in paragraph 6 that the boys from Oldtown were eager to hear the news.

Story text in paragraph 5: It was clear that the boy could not find his dog. He called and called for Raz for two days, but Raz did not come.

Statements identifying evidence:

4. It states in paragraph 5 he called and called for Raz for two days.

5. It states in paragraph 5 that the boy called and called for Raz for two days, but Raz did not come.

6. Raz was lost for two days. It states in paragraph 5 that for two days Raz did not come.

Story text in paragraph 8: Taffy drove across town to visit her grandmother.

Statements identifying evidence:

7. It states in paragraph 8 Taffy drove across town to visit her grandmother.

8. It states in paragraph 8 that Taffy drove across town to visit her grandmother.

9. It states in paragraph 8 that Taffy's grandmother lived across town.

END OF LESSON 105

A Connect each figure of speech with the correct sentence.

1. as tough as nails • • The bird grabbed a worm so fast, you could hardly see it. The bird was ___ .

2. lightning fast • • She thought the lamp was an original, but there were thousands of copies. The lamp was ___ .

3. as busy as a bee • • I couldn't believe Rene couldn't follow the plan. The plan was very obvious. It was ___ .

4. as clean as a whistle • • Doesn't he ever stop working? He's always on the move, doing something. He is ___ .

5. as common as dirt • • The plastic is very thin, but you can hit it with a hammer and not make a mark on it. It is ___ .

6. as plain as day • • After he showered and changed his clothes, I couldn't believe how spotless he looked. He was ___ .

B CITE EVIDENCE IN LITERARY TEXTS

You're going to learn more about quoting evidence from a story.

The story text in paragraph 8:

Marla said, "We have visited the best zoos in the country."

When you state evidence from the story:

a. Marla states in paragraph 8, "We have visited the best zoos in the country."

 If you want to make clear who "we" are, you could write sentence b.

b. Marla states in paragraph 8 that her family had "visited the best zoos in the country."

In sentence b, the words "her family" are used instead of "we." You can change or add words to make the full meaning of the quote clear.

Place quote marks and capital letters in these statements that identify evidence from the story.

Story text in paragraph 7: Linda said, "Things like that always happen."

Statements identifying evidence:

1. Linda states in paragraph 7 things like that always happen.

2. Linda states in paragraph 7 that things like that always happen.

3. In paragraph 7, Linda told Marc that things like that always happen.

Story text in paragraph 5:

White-Tip had grown into a strong, healthy wolf. Every few days, he would go back to the old routine—the lake in the morning and the hill in the evening. He told himself he was going there for food.

4. It states in paragraph 5 that White Tip went back to the old routine—the lake in the morning and the hill in the evening.

5. It states in paragraph 5 he told himself he was going there for food.

Story text in paragraph 4:

He told Milt, "It didn't hurt the bike at all, but I'm a wreck. I probably won't be biking for the next couple of years, and I thought you might want to use my bike."

6. It states in paragraph 4 that Fred told Milt that he wouldn't be biking for the next couple of years.

7. Fred hurt himself so badly that he wouldn't be able to bike for a long time. He told Milt in paragraph 4 I thought you might want to use my bike.

8. Fred told Milt in paragraph 4 that it didn't hurt the bike at all.

END OF LESSON 106

A CITE EVIDENCE IN LITERARY TEXTS

> Use quote marks to identify evidence that comes from a quote in the story. Another way to say **identify** evidence is to say **cite** evidence. You are learning how to **cite** evidence from a story.
>
> **The story text in paragraph 5:** Micha said, "I don't want to go with you."
>
> **Statements citing evidence:**
>
> a. **Micha stated in paragraph 5, "I don't want to go with you."**
> In sentence a, the evidence quote is the same as the quote in the story.
>
> b. **Micha stated in paragraph 5 that she didn't "want to go with [Isabel]."**
> In sentence b, the word "Isabel" is used instead of "you."
>
> c. **It states in paragraph 5 that "[Micha didn't] want to go with [Isabel]."**
> In sentence c, the words "Micha didn't" are used instead of "I don't."
> You can replace a word in a quote with a word that makes the meaning fit your sentence. You mark changed words with brackets [ ]. The new word must mean exactly the same thing as the word it replaced.

Place quote marks and capital letters in these statements that identify evidence from the story.

The story text in paragraph 6:

Laurel said, "No, Marc. You got me to be your girlfriend because I wanted to be your girlfriend."

Statements citing evidence:

1. Laurel states in paragraph 5 that Marc got her to be his girlfriend because she wanted to be his girlfriend.

2. Laurel tells Marc in paragraph 5 you got me to be your girlfriend because I wanted to be your girlfriend.

Story text in paragraph 4:

"I don't think you should drive home," Mike said. "You should not be driving. I'll take you where you want to go."

Statements citing evidence:

3. In paragraph 4, Mike stated that the old man should not be driving.

4. In paragraph 4, Mike told the old man I don't think you should drive home.

5. Mike states in paragraph 4 that he will take the old man where he wants to go.

Story text in paragraph 5:

John felt very uncomfortable sitting next to a person who didn't smell very good, whose clothes were tattered, and whose cough was so bad that the person obviously should not be on a subway or near other people.

Statements citing evidence:

6. It states in paragraph 5 that Murry's cough was so bad that he obviously should not be on a subway or near other people.

7. It states in paragraph 5 that John thought that Murry's cough was so bad that he should not be on a subway or near other people.

B Underline each figure of speech and tell what it means.

1. When Rosco goes to bed, he sleeps like a log.

2. I sometimes don't know when she leaves the room because she is as quiet as a mouse.

3. Mr. Jackson is as straight as an arrow.

4. Don't be fooled by her; she is a phony baloney.

END OF LESSON 107

A CITE EVIDENCE IN LITERARY TEXTS

> You're going to learn more about citing evidence from a story. Sometimes the evidence you put in quotes also has a quote. The quote mark for a quote inside a quote is only one mark.
>
> "When he said 'now,' he meant now."
>
> 'Now' is a quote inside another quote, so it has only one mark, called a "single quote." The double mark is called a "double quote."

Place quote marks and capital letters in these statements that identify evidence from the story. Make sure to include the single quotes.

The story text in paragraph 12:

He was watching television, and he saw someone he knew. He told Linda about it, and she said, "Oh, come on. It can't be him."

Statements citing evidence:

1. It states in paragraph 12 that Tony saw someone he knew. He told Linda about it, and she said, Oh, come on. It can't be him.

2. It states in paragraph 12 that Tony was watching television, and he saw someone he knew.

Story text in paragraph 11:

Then something deep and dark inside Josh said, "Even if it happens, maybe it would have happened anyhow."

Statements citing evidence:

3. It states in paragraph 11 then something deep and dark inside Josh said Even if it happens, maybe it would have happened anyhow.

4. It states in paragraph 11 that Josh felt something inside him say maybe it would have happened anyhow.

5. It states in paragraph 11 it would have happened anyhow.

6. Josh told May with certainty that he controlled the future. But in paragraph 11 it states that something deep and dark inside Josh said even if it happens, maybe it would have happened anyhow.

END OF LESSON 108

Name _____

110

A USE GREEK OR LATIN ROOTS AS CLUES TO MEANING

1. circ

2. dict

B For each sentence, write the best word for the blank.

verdict	dictate	circulate
circus	circumstance	circumference
dictionary	dictator	predict

1. I did not agree with the _____ of the judge.

2. The teacher _____ the words we were to write.

3. She measured the diameter and _____ of the circle.

4. It took more than an hour to describe all the _____ that led to the accident.

5. They stood on street corners and _____ papers that explained the new law.

6. The doctor told him that his blood was not _____ well.

7. I didn't know what the word meant so I looked it up in the _____ .

END OF LESSON 110

114 Name _____

A USE GREEK OR LATIN ROOTS AS CLUES TO MEANING

struct – build
vis – see

B For each sentence, write the best word for the blank.

> obstructing   visualize   televised
> reconstruct   construction   vision
> revise   instruction

1. There was a lot of _____ on the highways.

2. Our dog has lost most of his _____. He walks into things.

3. They plan to _____ the old Bunner building. It is falling down.

4. James was guilty of _____ the police investigation.

5. She provided very good _____ on how to remodel old buildings.

6. The game on Saturday will be _____. We can watch it from home.

7. It's time to _____ the book on good restaurants in the city. Some that were good are not so good anymore. And we have a lot of new good restaurants.

8. We tried to _____ the animals Mrs. Gally described.

END OF LESSON 114

Name _____

122

A In the box, write the number of the first paragraph in the story that answers each question. Then write the answer to the question.

1. Who are the two main characters of the story? ☐
_____

2. What special talent did Josh believe he had? ☐
_____

3. What was the first event that made Josh believe he had this talent? ☐
_____

4. How many more times did something similar happen to Josh? ☐
_____

5. Who was the first person Josh told about his special talent? ☐
_____

6. What example did Josh tell her about to prove he had a special talent? ☐
_____

7. What bet did Josh make with Linda to prove he had the special talent? ☐
_____

8. How hard did Josh work to try to win his bet? ☐
_____

9. What month was it when Linda talked to Josh again about outcome of the bet? ☐
_____

10. What reason did Josh give for not believing that he lost the bet? ☐
_____

END OF LESSON 122

124 Name _____

A Underline the figure of speech in each sentence. On the line below, write what the figure of speech means.

1. Joe wore his new tie and sport jacket. He said, "I am the best thing since sliced bread."
   _____

2. The children decided to make a garden, but after working a little more than an hour, they decided they bit off more than they could chew.
   _____

3. Mary tried to explain what her vacation plans were, but I still don't know what she is doing. She just beats around the bush.
   _____

4. The mechanic kept looking under the hood of the car, but the problem was with a tire. The mechanic was barking up the wrong tree.
   _____

END OF LESSON 124

Name _____ **126**

A **Underline the figure of speech in each sentence. On the line below, write what the figure of speech means.**

1. Fran tries to explain things, but it takes forever because she just beats around the bush.
   _____

2. Andy lost his watch. He keeps looking in his house for it. I think that he's barking up the wrong tree.
   _____

3. Linda is very self-centered. She thinks she is the greatest thing since sliced bread.
   _____

4. Ursula didn't study for the test until last night. Then she tried to catch up, but she bit off more than she could chew.
   _____

5. I'll never be able to afford a Bumpo. That brand costs an arm and a leg.
   _____

6. I can never talk to Marla without getting into an argument. She argues about anything at the drop of a hat.
   _____

7. We planned the field trip to the zoo for Monday, but now Monday doesn't work. It's time to go back to the drawing board.
   _____

8. His brother called him many times over the last week. Finally, his brother left the message, "The ball is in your court."
   _____

END OF LESSON 126

A. Draw a line to connect the right meaning with each figure of speech.

Figure of Speech	Meaning
1. beat around the bush	best thing you can find
2. costs an arm and a leg	going in the wrong direction
3. barking up the wrong tree	fail to make a point
4. at the drop of a hat	it's your turn
5. best thing since sliced bread	take on a project you are not able to finish
6. back to the drawing board	start over
7. bite off more than you can chew	costs a lot
8. ball is in your court	instantly

END OF LESSON 127

128

A — Under the figure of speech in each item. Write what the figure of speech means on the line below.

1. Mario's light was out. He changed the bulb twice, but the light still didn't work. Ella told him that he was barking up the wrong tree. The problem was in the wiring.
   _____

2. Marla wanted to tell Jason that she didn't want to go to the dance with him. But she just beat around the bush. She told him she couldn't dance and never got around to telling him that she really didn't want to go with him.
   _____

3. Mrs. Johnson dropped her antique glass and broke it. She was so upset with herself. Then she thought to herself, *I shouldn't cry over spilled milk.*
   _____

4. The men were in a hurry to get the job done. Instead of using a small paint brush for trim and a roller brush for large areas, they used a roller brush for everything. The paint job was a mess. That's what happens when you cut corners.
   _____

5. They discussed what they would do if their plan failed. Finally Tino asked, "What will we do if we can't raise all the money we need?"
   Ginger said, "We'll cross that bridge when we come to it."
   _____

6. Molly told her mother she was sure she was going to get an A on the test. Her mother said, "Don't count your chickens before they hatch."
   _____

7. Peg thought Bill was the best thing since sliced bread. She thought he was the smartest, best-looking, and kindest person she knew.
   _____

8. The Johnsons started remodeling their garage over the weekend. They thought they could do it themselves, but they bit off more than they could chew.
   _____

END OF LESSON 128

129

A Underline the figure of speech in each item. Write what the figure of speech means on the line below.

1. Fred kept trying to use a big wrench to unscrew the pipes. He put so much pressure on a pipe that it broke. After he cleaned up the mess, he said, "Live and learn."
   _____

2. Just as Ann was getting ready to leave, there was a knock on the back door. Before she could answer it, the front doorbell rang. Almost at the same time, somebody called her from upstairs. She shrugged and said, "When it rains, it pours."
   _____

3. Talbot had been living in London, England for ten years. When he talked of home, though, he was referring to the place he came from, where his parents still lived. His new friends knew that home is where the heart is.
   _____

4. People considered her very beautiful, but beauty is only skin deep. She didn't have very many friends.
   _____

END OF LESSON 129

Name _____   130

A **Underline the figure of speech in each item. Write what the figure of speech means on the line below.**

1. After she was made very famous by Mr. Briggs, she fired him. Now she is not very famous at all. Her friend reminded her, "Don't bite the hand that feeds you."
   _____

2. They wanted us to do the work, but they didn't want to pay us. They didn't seem to know that you can't have your cake and eat it, too.
   _____

3. He tried to describe the summer home and its surroundings, but he couldn't seem to put his thoughts into words. He finally showed us a picture, and we agreed that a picture is worth a thousand words.
   _____

4. Their daughter took a job on a tour ship, and they didn't hear from her for weeks. One day her mother complained about not hearing from her. Her father said, "No news is good news."
   _____

5. Scott was reading a history book, and he observed that a lot of inventions were made when people faced a problem they couldn't solve. For example, people needed to get places faster, so they invented the train, then the automobile, then the airplane. His mother said, "That's what happens. Necessity is the mother of invention."
   _____

END OF LESSON 130

131 Name _____

A Draw a line to connect the right meaning with each figure of speech.

Figure of Speech	Meaning
1. beat around the bush	best thing you can find
2. barking up the wrong tree	don't assume a good outcome
3. best thing since slice bread	fail to make a point
4. bite off more than you can chew	skip steps
5. don't count your chickens before the hatch	take on a project you are not able to finish
6. cut corners	instantly
7. at the drop of a hat	going in the wrong direction

B COMPARE AND CONTRAST VARIETIES OF ENGLISH

> Different language is used for different situations. The examples below are numbered from most informal to most polite.
>
> 1. Shut up!
> 2. Be quiet!
> 3. Please be quiet!
> 4. Would you please quiet down, so we can hear the sounds of nature?

Lesson 131

Number these expressions from most informal to most polite, 1 is most informal and 4 is most polite.

Set A

____ Stop running, please.

____ Would you please stop running?

____ Quit it!

____ Stop running!

Set B

____ Huh?

____ Excuse me?

____ What?

____ I'm sorry, I'm not sure I understand.

Set C

____ Of course!

____ Indubitably!

____ Ya betcha!

____ Sure!

Set D

____ Please tell me if you are going to be late.

____ Hurry up!

____ You need to pick up your pace if you're going to make it on time!

____ Get a wiggle on!

Set E

____ Would you please depart the premises!

____ Please leave!

____ Leave us alone!

____ Get out of here!

END OF LESSON 131

132 Name _____

A **Number these expressions from most informal to most polite. 1 is most informal and 4 is most polite.**

Set A

____ Would you please come inside?

____ Please come in.

____ Get your sorry self in here!

____ Get in here!

Set B

____ Would you please say that again?

____ Huh?

____ Excuse me?

____ What was that?

Set C

____ Please be quiet!

____ Would you please quiet down, so we can hears the sounds of nature?

____ Shut up!

____ Be quiet!

Set D

____ Please tell me if you are going to be late.

____ Hurry up!

____ You need to pick up your pace if you're going to make it on time!

____ Get a move on!

Set E

____ Of course!

____ Inevitably!

____ Okey dokey!

____ Sure!

INDEPENDENT WORK

B **Number these expressions from most informal to most polite. 1 is most informal and 4 is most polite.**

Set A

_____ Stop running, please.

_____ Would you please stop running?

_____ Quit it!

_____ Stop running!

Set B

_____ Huh?

_____ Excuse me?

_____ What?

_____ I'm sorry, I'm not sure I understand.

Set C

_____ Of course.

_____ Indubitably.

_____ Ya betcha!

_____ Sure.

END OF LESSON 132

133

INDEPENDENT WORK

A Number these expressions from most informal to most polite. 1 is most informal and 4 is most polite.

Set A

____ Be quiet, please!

____ Would you please quiet down, so we can hear the sounds of nature?

____ Shut up!

____ Be quiet!

Set B

____ Please tell me if you are going to be late.

____ Hurry up!

____ You need to pick up your pace if you're going to make it on time.

____ Get a move on!

Set C

____ Of course!

____ Inevitably!

____ Okey dokey!

____ Sure!

END OF LESSON 133